DEVELOPMENTS IN THE BALTIC MARITIME MARKETPLACE

Business 06103

SEVEN DAY LOAN

This book is to be returned on
or before the date stamped below

−3 NOV 2003

−4 DEC 2003

−2 3 FEB 2004
−9 MAR 2004

UNIVERSITY OF PLYMOUTH

PLYMOUTH LIBRARY

Tel: (01752) 232323
This book is subject to recall if required by another reader
Books may be renewed by phone
CHARGES WILL BE MADE FOR OVERDUE BOOKS

Developments in the Baltic Maritime Marketplace

Edited by
MICHAEL ROE
Centre for International Shipping and Transport
University of Plymouth

Ashgate

Aldershot • Brookfield USA • Singapore • Sydney

Published by
Ashgate Publishing Limited
Gower House
Croft Road
Aldershot
Hants GU11 3HR
England

Ashgate Publishing Company
Old Post Road
Brookfield
Vermont 05036
USA

British Library Cataloguing in Publication Data

Developments in the Baltic maritime marketplace. -
    (Plymouth studies in contemporary shipping)
    1. Shipping - Baltic Sea
    I. Roe, Michael, 1954-
    387.5 ' 0916334

Library of Congress Catalog Card Number: 97-74454

ISBN 1 84014 169 7

Printed and bound by Athenaeum Press, Ltd.,
Gateshead, Tyne & Wear.

Contents

Acknowledgements

It would be nice to claim that this volume was entirely down to me, but clearly that would not be true. Lots of others helped me along the way. My colleagues in Gdansk, in particular Janusz Zurek, but also all the other Polish authors, should be thanked for their efforts. Without them the text would have been very thin. My colleagues in Plymouth also merit consideration including Kevin Cullinane as Head of the Centre, Neal Toy as facilitator, particularly with respect to visitors, and Marie Bendell who provided around half of the word processing and a considerable amount of common sense. Ex-students at Plymouth - Chris Dent and Marius Rostock Olsen provided high quality research material with which to work, whilst Gillian Ledger provided her last of many year's contributions to the Centre through additional word processing and a considerable amount of down to earth advice. Sarah Markham and Anne Keirby at Ashgate have been endlessly patient yet again and made the whole process virtually painless. Various individuals in Poland also helped the Editor in a variety of ways but I will feature only two. In particular, the staff at the Hotel Europejski in Warsaw provided traditional East European hospitality just at a time when I thought the old traditions had been lost; whilst the help of Magdalena Zalinska in Lodz in providing access to the real Poland will not be forgotten.

Finally, as ever, thanks must go to two football teams that rarely get a look in at an academic (or practical) level - the nearest; Plymouth Argyle - and the best; Charlton Athletic; and in particular to Liz, Joe and Siân who act as my very own personal supporters club.

Introduction

Michael Roe
Institute of Marine Studies
University of Plymouth

This text is the second in a series of volumes produced in collaboration between the Institute of Maritime Transport and Seaborne Trade at the University of Gdansk in Poland and the Institute of Marine Studies at the University of Plymouth in the United Kingdom. It attempts to build upon the first volume of papers which emerged in 1996 which concentrated upon the early developments in the maritime sector in the Baltic region with particular reference to the changing circumstances that have affected the ports and shipping sector in Poland. In this volume, the focus of attention moves to the changes within the marketplace for the maritime sector ranging across a diverse number of topics including both maritime and land based transport infrastructure.

The situation in the maritime sector in Poland has continued to change very rapidly in terms of attitude and the growth of the private sector, and there have also been a succession of changes in the state sector relating in particular to the status of port authorities and their ultimate ownership. However, at the same time, despite this rate of change there remains a large part of the maritime sector which is resistant to the developments in the industry and which remains locked into the old attitude which centres around a failure to recognise market developments and the need to take a positive and practical stance to customers and competitors if the industry is to survive. At the moment these ex (or in some cases still) state-owned industries remain effectively protected from the dangers of the free market, but for how long?

It is within this context that these papers have been produced to review the situation as seen by those in the industry, academic commentators outside and also from a west European perspective from the United Kingdom.

The first paper by Dobrowolski and Zurek provides a basic introduction into the earlier phases of the economic reconstruction programme that was

1

introduced in Poland following the economic, political and social changes that took place through the 1980s and culminated in the dramatic events of 1989 and 1990. It acts as a forerunner to the discussion in subsequent papers which examines the implications for the maritime sector, of the transformation in the economy that has occurred so far. The authors are both from the Institute of Maritime Transport and Seaborne Trade at the University of Gdansk. Professor Janusz Zurek is the current Director of the Institute.

The second paper, by Kryzystof Dobrowolski alone, examines the processes which have been adopted in Poland to transform the enterprises of the economy into a privatised sector and in so doing provides the basis for the discussion of the maritime sector that follows it.

The paper by Konrad Misztal of the Institute of Maritime Transport and Seaborne Trade takes a specific and detailed look at the situation within Polish seaports and the attempts beginning to be made to transform them as a consequence of the political, social and economic changes of the 1980s and 1990s. In itself, it provides a unique insight into a sector that has been largely ignored in the western press and other published output but which has the potential to develop into a formidable force in the future as transit ports for a recovering and developing Russia and Former Soviet Union.

Janusz Zurek, we have already noted, is the current Director of the Institute in Gdansk and has a long and distinguished history of teaching and research in the field of maritime, and particularly shipping, business. The paper he presents on "The privatisation of Polish shipping: present situation and development" is an analysis of the situation up to around the beginning of 1995 in the Polish shipping industry with respect to the privatisation process and in particular the events at the state liner operator, Polish Ocean Lines of Gdynia.

The next paper by Krzyzanowski and Skurewicz is a short analysis of the effects of market forces upon the Polish shipping industry at a time of major transformation and in particular looks at the developments in this sector in the early years of economic change around the period of 1989 to 1993. Both authors are attached to the Maritime Research Institute in Gdansk which operates separate from, but in close collaboration with the Institute of Maritime Transport and Seaborne Trade. Krystyna Wasilewska is also from the latter and in her paper on "Poland in the Southern Baltic transit market" presents an analysis of the role of Polish ports and shipping as part of the Trans European Motorway system linking many of the countries of eastern and southern Europe with those of Scandinavia. The significant issues that stem from this transit role for the maritime sector are discussed in the light of changing economic pressures and market demands. This paper is particularly valuable as it presents one of the few analyses of the role of transit in east Europe and the impact of infrastructural developments - particularly road developments - on the ports and shipping sectors.

Tadeusz Lodykowski's paper on "The influence of changes in East European countries upon their merchant fleets" presents an exhaustive longitudinal study of the changes that have taken place within the east European shipping industry, developing the theme from activities and events in the past, through the current phase with a look at the factors and issues that will be important for the sector throughout the region in the future. The author is also attached to the Institute of Maritime Studies and Seaborne Trade at the University of Gdansk.

Michal Rosa looks at the impact of Poland's political and economic changes upon the shipping sector, from the perspective of the industry taking a practical view as the former Vice-Director of Polish Ocean Lines - the principle state liner carrier - and examining the impacts of change just prior to the major structural developments in the company in 1990-1991.

The final paper from Poland is by Konrad Misztal of the Institute in Gdansk University and presents a brief look at the role and activities of Polish seaports in the new environment since the economic changes of both the 1980s and 1990s. The final two papers come from research into the Baltic maritime scene conducted at the Institute of Marine Studies at the University of Plymouth. The first, by Christopher Dent (now of Thomas Miller / UK P&I Club, London) and Michael Roe, research professor at the Centre for International Shipping & Transport takes a long and detailed look at the legal and regulatory issues that have emerged following the sinking of the Estonia in 1994 in the Baltic Sea. In particular it concentrates upon the growth in the roll on roll off ferry industry in the Baltic and the failure of regulatory practice and legislation to keep up with developments in the industry. To illustrate these problems graphically, the case of the Estonia sinking is used with particular emphasis on the role of the P&I Clubs and the classification societies in enforcing and encouraging safety.

The final paper is another extended analysis from researchers at the Institute of Marine Studies at the University of Plymouth, looking at the Baltic region as a location for the market and transport of metals with particular reference to the role of Russia and the other states of the Former Soviet Union. This is a market that has been largely neglected in terms of analysis and this paper thus presents one of the few attempts to gather together information on the sector since the major political, social and economic upheavals of the late 1980s.

The whole sector of the east European shipping industry is one that has been largely neglected by the research community until very recently and it is hoped that this volume of papers, in combination with the earlier "Shipping in the Baltic Region" comprising a series of papers from the same sources, can go some way towards filling the gap in the literature for an industrial sector that is both sizeable and significant. Research into the maritime industries of the region continues at both establishments and a number of future volumes are already planned and in the process of development. The continued assistance of colleagues in Gdansk needs to be noted and in particular the efforts provided by   Professor Janusz Zurek, as Director of the group, without which this, previous and future volumes would never be completed.   The developments which continue to occur within the industry and region are unlikely to slow down and as such the continued need for research will form the basis for the extended collaboration that will persist.   These are exciting times in the industry in Poland and the other countries of the region in all sectors but in particular those where the state is attempting to loosen its hold but where the pressing economic difficulties make this problematic.   Research efforts in the immediate future will attempt to follow these activities through the publication of increasing numbers of texts in this series.

Those readers who find the area of particular interest and wish to follow the research activities further are encouraged to contact the editor in Plymouth or Professor Zurek in Gdansk, both of whom would be happy to discuss developments and ideas concerning the sector and the region.

The basic assumptions and realisation of the Polish economic reconstruction programme

Krzysztof Dobrowolski and Janusz Zurek
Institute of Maritime Transport and Seaborne Trade
University of Gdansk

Abstract

This paper provides a basic introduction into the earlier phases of the economic reconstruction programme that was introduced in Poland following the economic, political and social changes that took place through the 1980s and culminated in the dramatic events of 1989 and 1990. It acts as a forerunner to the discussion in subsequent papers which examines the implications for the maritime sector, of the transformation in the economy that has occurred so far.

Introduction

Poland's economy is at present experiencing a phase of profound structural changes stemming primarily from proprietary, organisational and legal transformation, sizeable alterations in the state/enterprise management relationship and within the enterprise itself, and also within the sphere of economic-financial regulatory mechanisms organised by the state.

The market is becoming the basic motivational force of structural changes within the economy. The role of the state has altered to become one that concentrates upon legislative control and regulatory functions, as well as, to a certain extent, functions supporting the market mechanism from the financial-organisational side.

Changes in the legal-economic regulatory mechanisms are becoming particularly important in the light of Poland's likely future membership of the European Union. The process of adaptation is by no means easy, requiring far reaching changes in the construction of law, as well as the introduction of new economic rules and instruments corresponding to the requirements of the international regulatory system.

The reconstruction programme

The transformation of the system towards a market economy is becoming a tremendous challenge for Poland's economy. The programme for this transformation was formulated in the economic agenda proclaimed by the government on 12 October 1989, and introduced on 1 January 1990. This was a complex programme of stabilisation and planned changes agreed with the International Monetary Fund.

The following tasks were the primary contents of the programme:

- a change in the legal system creating suitable conditions for
  economic reconstruction;
- the creation of suitable conditions for balancing the budget;
- the introduction of a reliable monetary credit system;
- stabilising the currency exchange rate and introducing convertibility
  of currency;
- introduction of the principles of liberalised price setting;
- the introduction of a restricted incomes policy;
- reconstruction of the banking system, the efficient operation of which
  is a basic condition for normal functioning of the economy;
- reconstruction of ownership relationships, which constitute a basic
  element in improving the effectiveness of the economy.

The central concept of the programme was mainly directed towards the suppression of inflation and stabilisation of the economy and constitutes the starting point for clarifying the functions of institutions and rules of the market. Generally speaking it was a compact programme, but primarily a logical one affording the chance to transform a centrally planned economy into a market one. During the period of this economic transformation, fulfilment of many elements of the programme was achieved thus noticeably drawing Poland closer to the western European market economy.

Within the framework of the programme outlined, the mechanisms of foreign trade underwent profound reconstruction. An important role in this mechanism was played by the initial stable currency exchange rate of 9,500 zloties/US dollar. Simultaneously, convertibility of the zloty was introduced in Poland, thus facilitating the active participation of Polish companies in international trade, without the necessity to have assembled large hard currency resources. In accordance with the currency laws, banks were obliged to sell foreign currency to Polish citizens with few restrictions, the main one being the exception of foreign currency assets, as well as transport, forwarding and insurance services. Simultaneously, all economic subjects were obliged to sell all currency returns acquired from exports and other sources, to foreign exchange banks. The extensive system of direct and intermediate subsidising of exports and that of exchange retention quotas, was abolished.

External safeguarding of changes in the functioning of foreign trade was achieved through a stabilisation fund of 1 million US dollars. Also introduced was the principle of depositing in the bank a sum amounting to 10% of the value of the currency acquired, this not being subject to interest.

Substantial changes were introduced into the policy connected with the transferable rouble. A new rate was fixed - 1 transferable rouble = 2,100 zloties. Due to the differences in trade exchange with countries of the former "first payment area", mainly with the Soviet Union, the zloty/transferable rouble rate of exchange was differentiated in mid 1990. For trade transactions covered by trade agreements, the previous rate was maintained, but for other accounts a new rate of exchange of 1,000 zloties/transferable rouble was introduced.

Changes in the exchange rate policy were accompanied by similar ones in the customs system and import/export turnover taxes. A single customs tariff for all imports was introduced, whether business or otherwise, abolishing that previously in force. Reductions and allowances were greatly restricted. The principles of foreign trade exchange were largely liberalised, considerably restricting the range of licensing of imports and exports.

A very important factor was the acceptance of the principle that any enterprise could conduct foreign trade transactions without having to take advantage of the agency of special foreign trade centres - i.e. FTOs.

Essential changes in the principles of trade with countries which used to belong to the former "first payment area", took place in 1991. The basis of mutual settlement was agreed as convertible currency whilst the transferable rouble was eliminated as a conversion unit. The principles of mutual trade exchange with the individual countries belonging to the former Council for Mutual Economic Assistance (CMEA) were settled under separate bilateral agreements.

The next essential change, introduced in 1991, was the devaluation of the zloty by 16.8% in May. The stiff zloty/US dollar rate of exchange, maintained from January 1990 at a steady level, became a barrier for firms exporting their products and services. The reason for this was inflation, resulting in the rate of exchange of the zloty which had been established 18 months previously, becoming increasingly less profitable for exporters. The principles behind the exchange rate choice changed with the devaluation as it was now to be set in relation to other currencies in addition to the US dollar. As from 17 May 1991, the basis for calculating the exchange rate has constituted a basket of currencies consisting of 45% US$, 35% DM, 10% £, 5% French Franc and 5% Swiss Franc. The currency basket was initially stable at 11,100 zloties/US dollar, meaning that depending upon fluctuations in the rate of the US dollar to other currencies, the exchange rates of all currencies, including the US dollar, might change but the value of the whole basket would correspond with the fixed level. In 1991, there were essential changes in the law regulating the activities of companies with a share of foreign capital. The Agency for Foreign Investments was wound up, some of its responsibilities being taken over by the Ministry of Privatisation. A new institution engaged mainly in promotion, was also established.

The previously binding threshold of capital commitment for a foreign partner, amounting to a minimum of 50,000 US dollars, was waived. The areas of the economy in which commencement of foreign activity depended upon state permission, were cut considerably. Those who might apply for tax reductions were those who had invested capital of not less than 2 million ECU and satisfied in addition, one of the following conditions:

    -they invested in areas particularly prone to unemployment;
    -they launched new technologies;
    -the company's exports amounted to at least 20% of turnover.

In accordance with the new, updated law, a foreign partner was afforded unlimited possibilities of transferring profits abroad. The aim of introducing these changes was to attract serious investors, prepared to launch substantial investments.

As from 1990, essential changes have been introduced into the system of taxation. The purpose of the changes was to standardise the principles of taxation in all sectors of the economy, irrespective of the type of ownership, structure of the enterprises or their particular characteristics. In general, the taxation policy has become more stringent, due to the raising of the basic rate of turnover tax to 20% (previously 15%), extending the range of application of this tax, and the elimination of numerous tax reductions. Credit, monetary and budget policies have also become more stringent.

As regards credit policy, the aim was to maintain the interest rate for loans and savings accounts. The decisions concerning loan agreements with interest set at fixed rates, were annulled. In consequence, as from January 1990, variable rates of interest on loans were introduced, depending upon the level of inflation. In the first half year, interest rates on credits were fixed for monthly periods and as from July, annual rates of interest on loans were introduced. Interest on savings accounts was changed with the same frequency.

Important instruments in credit policies introduced by the central bank were the rate of interest for refinanced loans and the rediscount rate. The limiting of loans was maintained to a certain extent, the financial liquidity of the commercial banks being influenced by means of the level of the compulsory rate of reserves in the central bank.

Changes in credit policies also consisted of the abolition of preference for the state sector in respect of loans, interest on such and repayment terms.

The next element in the monetary-credit policy was assumption of the principle that the budget deficit could not be covered by the issue of fiat money (in the form of interest free credit for the budget) by the Polish National Bank. The introduction of a balanced budget policy over a long period of time was assumed, a budget deficit being foreseen in the initial quarters of 1990, which was to be eliminated in the fourth quarter. The financing of the deficit was to come from the following sources:

> -in the first quarter by means of commercial credit negotiated outside the Polish National Bank;
> -in the second quarter by issuing short term Treasury bills on which interest was to be paid.

One source of financing a budget deficit could be the issuing of Treasury bonds, purchased voluntarily by banks and other economic units, as well as Polish persons. The Minister of Finance may also negotiate loans with commercial banks, but within limits fixed by law.

Stringent restrictions were placed on payments from wages funds in state owned enterprises, as well as public and non commercial partnerships. No restrictions were applied to companies in which foreign capital was engaged.

In 1991, added to the law on taxation of wage increases, was a record on the basis of which trading and non-commercial partnerships were to pay lower taxes than state owned enterprises. The scale of reduction of taxation depended upon the amount of non-private capital engaged in the company. Companies in which 50% to 80% of the contributions or shares belong to the Treasury, state owned enterprises, communal or inter-parishional units, paid 50% of the sum due for tax. In relation to companies in which the non-private capital exceeded 80%, the tax for extra-normative increases in salaries was reduced by 20%. These privileges were awarded to companies which did not adopt monopolistic practices and fulfilled their obligations in relation to the budget.

It was realised that conducting an active monetary credit policy was impossible without an overall reconstruction of the banking system. Thus, the reforms in the banking system commenced in 1989 and consisting in establishing a network of private commercial banks, opening the way for foreign banks, separating the budget from the central bank and transforming state-owned and state-owned co-operative banks into companies in which the Treasury would have a share. The central bank finally became an institution, the tasks of which were concentrated upon the control of the issue of money and the amount of money in circulation.

An important element in all the changes was the full liberalisation of prices. Administrative control of prices was only maintained in sensitive areas in the economy, or those important from the point of view of the public. This included the prices of coal, electricity, central heating and hot water, rents, public transport fares, medicines, pesticides, spirits and milk. The maintenance of price regulation in respect of these goods and services stemmed from the necessity to maintain, to a limited degree, subsidies, which formed an exception to the generally adopted economic principles.

Further price liberalisation took place in 1991 and the list of goods, the prices of which were controlled by the administration, was shortened. The system of payment for medicines was also reformed. The central system of distributing raw materials and other items and the regulation of other goods was simultaneously abolished.

Conclusions

Fulfilment of the reconstruction programme for the economy enabled stabilisation to be achieved over a longer period, reduction of the level of inflation, introduction of the mechanisms of competition and created the basis for further economic development.

The changes taking place have brought Poland's economy closer to the mechanisms of a market economy characteristic of economically developed countries. During this short period much has been done, but many problems remain to be solved. Further changes are required in the monetary credit policies, which should create conditions for increased investment demands, guaranteeing new jobs and thus counteracting the occurrence of recession. Efforts should also be concentrated upon increasing exports, this being an important element in the country's economic development as well as influencing improvement in the balance of payments structure. Another important problem is the level of the domestic debt occurring between enterprises, as well as between enterprises and banks, which is much more dangerous for the economy than the scale of budget deficit. The last of the important problems is that of foreign debt, the reduction of which is extremely difficult, as it necessitates strict regulation of the economy and its marked international expansion.

Privatisation of state owned enterprises in Poland's economy

Krzysztof Dobrowolski
Institute of Maritime Transport and Seaborne Trade
University of Gdansk

Abstract

This paper examines the processes which have been adopted in Poland to transform the enterprises of the economy into a privatised sector and in so doing provides the basis for the discussion of the maritime sector that follows in the next sections.

Introduction

The main aim of effecting changes of ownership in the economy is to increase the effectiveness of utilising existing resources. This aim can be achieved by the allocation of resources - carried out through the medium of the market, facilitating the free flow of capital - in undertakings displaying the most favourable income to expenditure ratio. Privatisation as such, will not increase the effectiveness of management but it is, however, a necessary requirement for its improvement, as it does away with the structural paradox of the system of the state-owned enterprise which the state manages alternately by administrative and civil-legal implements. By virtue of authority and rights of ownership, the state's powers and responsibilities cross and conflict, and consequently, the laws of ownership become obscure and as a result ineffective. In private enterprises there is a clear definition of the rights of ownership and clearly defined rights of established owners.

The essential aim of privatisation is also to integrate Poland's industry with the economy of Western Europe, by ensuring the same mechanisms that influence industry in the highly industrialised countries of the world are in operation there as well.

The process of privatising state owned enterprises is regulated by the rules of the law of 13.VII.1990. This law, together with executive acts, constitutes the legal basis for changes of ownership and comprehensively defines the legally permitted methods of privatising enterprises. The law foresees two basic procedures in changes of ownership: capital and direct (liquidational).

The capital method of privatising consists of the conversion - in the first stage - of a state owned enterprise into a joint stock company or one with limited responsibility. In view of the fact that at this stage, 100% of the shares of the company belong to the state, we have to deal with a change in the legal form of conducting economic activities, whereas there is no change in the form of ownership. This stage is frequently called the commercialisation of an enterprise. Established as the result of conversion, the joint stock company, with the state as sole shareholder, assumes all the rights and obligations of the enterprise, its closing balance sheet becoming the opening one for the company. In keeping with the provisions of the Privatisation Act, within the period of two years from the moment of converting the enterprise into a company (the registration of the company), the Minister of Privatisation should sell the company's shares to private persons i.e. carry out the actual privatisation. The statutory period of two years, counting from the moment of registering the company, exists to allow a detailed analysis of the legal standing of the company's property, its possible restructuring and assessment of assets in order to fix the sale price of shares. After fulfilling the requirements of the Securities Commission, the shares of the privatised company can once more be presented on the Warsaw Stock Exchange.

Direct privatisation consists of the liquidation of a state owned enterprise as a specific legal form and the management of the enterprise's estate by:

-sale;
-as a contribution to the company;
-renting it to the company.

The most popular method of privatisation within the process of winding up, is the establishment by the firm's employees, of trading companies, for the purpose of utilisation against payment by the company, of the fixed assets of the enterprise liquidated. In return for utilisation of the fixed assets, the company pays the costs of the lease and capital instalments to the Treasury and thus the assets leased become their property on conclusion of the term of the contract.

Direct (liquidational) privatisation, carried out on the basis of the law on privatisation of state owned enterprises, should be differentiated from the liquidation of enterprises for economic reasons, based upon the rules of the law on state owned enterprises. The basic difference stems from the purpose of the conversion. If the purpose of the conversion when liquidating an enterprise is that it, or its organised parts in their changed legal form, should further function, then, in the case of liquidation for economic reasons, the aim is to wind up the ineffective economic subject and the payment of its obligations with income gained from the sale of its property.

As the result of agreements drawn up within the so called "pact on the enterprise" during the process of transformation, towards the end of April 1993, the draft of a new law on privatisation of state owned assets was submitted to parliament. The draft upheld the existing methods of privatisation, although advantage was taken of almost three years experience in privatisation to define more clearly, many of the attestations enabling the univocal definition of the rights and obligations of the particular participants in the privatisation process. The new version of the privatisation law extends the range of rights of farm workers, farmers and fishermen directly connected with privatised enterprises.

In the six months following the coming into force of the new law on privatisation, the employees of the particular enterprises will have to state their choice of privatisation transformation (in exceptional circumstances, this period can be extended to nine months). Should no specific choice be made, the method of privatisation may be imposed.

W.Kaczmarek - Minister of Privatisation in Prime Minister W. Pawlak's government withdrew the draft of the new law on privatisation from parliament towards the end of October 1993. The draft is to be reconsidered in the Ministry of Privatisation.

Its results form the preliminary declaration of the new minister, that no general change will be introduced into the draft law on privatisation withdrawn from parliament but, what have been introduced on the other hand, are records formalising particular elements of the procedure of privatising enterprises, and

14

those regulating the sale of shares to domestic businessmen in instalments. As announced, the corrected draft of the law was submitted to Parliament at the beginning of 1994.

The Ministry of Privatisation has drawn up several programmes for the purpose of speeding up and improving the privatisation process:-

1. Programme for the quick sale of small and medium sized enterprises

Quick sales concern enterprises in various economic situations, which means departing from the primary principle of only privatising enterprises that attain good results. Privatisation in this manner, is carried out on the initiative of the programming authority, which chooses the enterprise and, by means of announcement in the press, tenders for buyers - primarily persons from Poland. The principle is to sell whole enterprises together with their commitments. Sale is based on the principle of tenders or auction, when the choice of the best offer embraces such proposals as e.g. the undertaking to carry out specific investments, employ a certain minimum number of workers, etc.

Following the choice of the preferred offer by the initiator's authority and fixing the detailed conditions of the transaction, the Minister of Privatisation takes the decision concerning winding up enterprises on the basis of art. 37 of the law on privatisation of state owned enterprises. The founder's authority then produces and processes the formal contract of sale.

The Ministry of Privatisation proposed that the founders adopt the following principles to finance transactions:

- part of the price of the sale, not less than 40%, should be paid in cash upon the drawing up of the purchase contract;
- the remainder may be paid in instalments over 4 years;
-the interest on the instalments to be paid should be calculated in accordance with the principles contained in the instructions of the Minister of Finance of 10.XI.1990 (up dated in May 1993).

It should be emphasised that in the case of a quick sale, the whole process of liquidation of the enterprise adopted in other methods of direct privatisation is not set in motion. The method of valuation of the enterprise is also simplified and retaining certain limits, is based upon the book value and annual profits. The aim of such solutions is to speed up the sale and substantially lower the costs. In view of the special credit facilities and simplified procedure, this method was initially available only for Polish citizens, but at present, in the case of a lack of Polish buyers, foreign investors are afforded the facilities when the offer is repeated.

2. Programme of sectoral privatisation

The idea of a sectoral privatisation consists of the concept of privatising whole branches of the economy as practice has shown that changes in the formula of ownership of a single enterprise (particularly when foreign capital is committed) may have an essential influence upon the market position of other enterprises functioning in the same economic sector. To assess the potential negative effects of such a situation, research has been carried out embracing all the enterprises belonging to a particular branch along with simulations of the economic impact. Based upon these studies, a privatisation strategy was worked out for the whole sector, or just for the leading enterprises of the branch. The following branches were included in the sectorial privatisation programme:

-building/construction
-cellulose/paper
-cement/limestone
-heavy chemicals
-confectionery
-cable and wire
-roller bearings
-electrical machinery and appliances
-furniture
-mechanical and electronic car parts
-machine tools
-footwear
-tyres and rubber goods
-breweries
-glass works
-telecommunications

Following the experience which was gained during the introduction of the particular sectoral programmes, the initial concept was modified. First and foremost, the number of sectoral programmes was cut substantially. In addition to this, regional programmes including privatising particular enterprises belonging to a specific economic branch and located in a specific region, were initiated. In the first phase, the programme embraced specific regions of southern and eastern Poland, in which privatisation processes had until then, proceeded most slowly.

3. The general privatisation programme
The general privatisation programme was drawn up for the purpose of:

-increasing the efficiency and value of several hundred Polish enterprises, by their commercialisation and the transfer of some of the shares to investment groups (National Investment Funds);
-the radical speeding up of changes in ownership in Poland and decentralisation as a prerequisite for increasing the capability of the economy to adapt to market demands;

16

-the facilitation and encouragement of all those who are of age to take part in the privatisation process through the medium of investment groups.

According to the programme assumptions, about 600 medium and large sized enterprises are to be transformed into joint stock companies with the state as the sole shareholder. An important element of the programme is the establishment of investment groups (from a dozen or so to several score), so called National Investment Funds. These groups have the form of "closed end funds" i.e. what is known in market economies as joint investment funds. They will originate as joint stock companies. The shares of enterprises transformed into joint stock companies with the state as the sole shareholder, will be divided as follows:

-33% of the shares of each company are to be transferred to one National Investment Fund, according to a pre-determined random sequence of choice:
-27% of the shares will be distributed between the remaining Funds;
-up to 15% of the shares will be handed over gratuitously to the company employees;
-25% of the shares will be held by the Treasury, to be handed over in the future to social insurance institutions which would contribute to an element of reform in this sector of the economy.

In accordance with the assumptions, the task of the National Investment Funds, as owners of the controlling interest, will be to bring about an increase in the market value of the assets of the particular companies. The National Investment Funds will be able to trade in shares, including the sale to third persons of controlling interest or smaller quantities.
Companies will be subject to restructuring processes and encouraged to take other steps improving their effectiveness, including:

-the drawing up of joint ventures or contracts of management with other thriving firms;
-the issue of successive shares which will be taken up by investment groups or third persons;
-the negotiating of loans for investment purposes;
-the introduction of shares into the Warsaw stock exchange.

To increase the effectiveness of decisions taken by the National Investment Fund, they will contain, through the mediation of the Ministry of Privatisation, contracts on the management of their controlling blocks of shares in companies, with competing, specialised managing firms, appointed by invited international tenders.
An essential element of the programme is the distribution of share certificates in the National Investment Funds amongst the adult Polish population. The share

certificates can then be exchanged for shares in any of the Funds. These shares can then be admitted to quotation at the Warsaw Stock Exchange.

In the first tranche of 200 enterprises, share certificates will be issued free to pensioners, retired employees and state employees; in the second tranche of 400 enterprises, share certificates will be issued after payment of a registration fee of about 10% of the average monthly salary, to all adult citizens in the country.

The programme of universal privatisation will enable rapid privatisation (without the need for preliminary evaluation) of a considerable number of large and medium sized enterprises of better than average financial situation. With the help of the best management experts available on the market, there will be an effective chance for the utilisation of foreign credit lines, new technologies and new market outlets and thus begin to play the role of the driving wheel of Poland's economy.

4. The privatisation restructuring programme

The main idea of the project leads to the emergence, by way of competition or tender, of groups of managers, who will prepare and carry out the restructuring plans for both joint stock companies with the state as the sole shareholder and state owned enterprises, and lead to their being privatised. A management group may constitute domestic and foreign legal or natural persons, hitherto existing boards of firms existing in the form of companies, groups of employees comprising a civil corporation, other enterprises etc.. The restructuring projects drawn up by these, will be assessed by the Ministry of Privatisation Competition Commission, the members of which will include representatives of the Ministry supervisory councils (workers' councils). The managerial group which works out the restructuring plan for a state owned enterprise that is highest appraised, will gain the right to sign a business contract which will also define the principles of remuneration. The most innovative element of such a contract is the part which makes the payment of commission for the restructuring subject to the difference between the value of the enterprise defined by the parties to the contract prior to the signing of the contract, and the price acquired from the sale of the enterprise after its restructuring. This means that the person, or group of persons, winning the contract will be paid according to normal managerial rates, negotiated with the supervisory council and receive additional payment equal to 30% of the difference between the sale price of the enterprise and its initial value, i.e. that negotiated at the time of signing the contract.

Fulfilment of the restructuring plan takes place under the supervision of the Ministry of Privatisation and supervisory council of the company that is being restructured.

5. Instalment share sales programme

This programme is directed at Poland's private capital and the management of state owned enterprises and is aimed at extending the share of these groups in the process of privatisation. This programme will include the privatisation of small and medium sized enterprises.

The first stage of privatisation will be transforming the enterprise into a joint stock company with the state as the sole shareholder. Then by inviting tenders, supplemented if needs be by auction, the purchaser(s) of the share(s) of the company sold emerge(s). A specified percentage of the shares will be reserved for the employees.

In view of the restricted funds at the disposal of domestic businessmen, only part of the price fixed for the share will be paid in cash over a period not longer than 10 years. The innovation will be that the purchaser will become the owner of the enterprise at the moment of signing the agreement and not after payment of the last instalment. The acceptance of such a solution demands that the interests of the Treasury be secured and this may assume various forms, e.g. a lien on the shares of the enterprise procured, mortgage on property, lien on other securities, mortgage on the personal property of the purchaser, bank guarantees, surety or contractual surety in the form of a declaration that speculation is not the intention of the purchaser.

The possibility of applying special conditions upon the payment of instalment by the purchaser (16-32 months), and also the payment of interest connected with purchase by deferred payments at the rate of refinancing credit, is taken into account. The rule would be to accept 100% of the rate of refinancing credit, whereas in the case of the purchaser's commitment to reinvest the reduction gained in the interest on the debt, it is proposed to lower the rate of refinancing credit to 50%.

Discussion

The last question of this paper is: what are the effects of converting state owned enterprises ?

On 1 August 1990, when the law on privatisation came into being and the process of changing of ownership commenced in Poland, there were 8,441 state owned enterprises. By the end of 1993 conversions of ownerships based on the privatisation law embraced 1,439 enterprises, or about 17%. In this period the Ministry had converted 522 enterprises into joint stock companies with the state as the sole shareholder, about 400 being destined for the Universal Privatisation Programme, and 100 totally or partially privatised, 917 privatised enterprises have been liquidated by taking advantage of the following statutory possibilities:

-sale (including the quick sale programme) - 139 enterprises
-contributing to the company - 41 enterprises
-handing over to the company for renting - 674 enterprises
-combined utilisation of several possibilities - 63 enterprises

By the end of December 1993, the process of direct privatisation was completed in the case of 707 enterprises, which constitutes about 77% of all enterprises privatised by this method.

In conclusion, it should be noted that the number of state owned enterprises in Poland's economy was reduced not only as the result of privatisation, but also liquidation for economic reasons, carried out on the basis of the law on state owned enterprises. Those put into liquidation on the basis of this law were primarily those enterprises not having paid their commitments to the budget for longer periods of time due to their poor economic/financial situation. By the end of December 1993, 1,082 enterprises had been subjected to liquidation for this reason, this process having been completed in the case of 172 enterprises (about 16%), and in the case of 242, bankruptcy proceedings had been set in motion. The essential barrier hindering completion of the process of liquidation, is the lack of demand for the remaining estate and property of these enterprises.

Based on the law of insolvency, bankruptcy proceedings were commenced in respect of a further 378 enterprises, whose obligations to creditors exceeded the value of their own estate.

263 enterprises were transferred to territorial authorities, thus becoming municipal enterprises. 1,595 state owned agricultural holdings were closed down, their estate being handed over to the Panstwowa Agencja Wlasnosci Rolnej Skarbu Panstwa.

Altogether about 4,757 state owned enterprises, i.e. about 56% of the initial number, were subjected to various types of conversion (privatisation, liquidation for economic reasons, bankruptcy, communalization).

Postscript

In the last few years since the beginning of 1994, the Universal Privatisation Programme has been modified substantially and the use of National Investment Funds at least temporarily abandoned to be replaced by selected privatisation of individual enterprises as and when circumstances allowed.

System transformation
in Poland's seaports

Konrad Misztal
Institute of Maritime Transport and Seaborne Trade
University of Gdansk

Abstract

This paper takes a specific and detailed look at the situation within Polish seaports and the attempts beginning to be made to transform them as a consequence of the political, economic and social changes of the 1980s and 1990s.

The change of the political-economic system in Poland demands profound and essential transformation of the system in the country's economy. The previous economic system in force during the period of "real socialism", based upon the centralised planned economy system, the basis of which constituted state owned production means, led to the far reaching monopolisation of economic activities and restriction of the independence of enterprises and their distancing from the free market.

In accordance with these principles, port services within Poland were developed with a structure mainly based on the state owned sector characterised by large monopolistic enterprises having at their disposal the sole rights to handle all commodities and arrange all ancillary activities. This resulted in the absorption of each of Poland's ports by one handling and management centre, these being the Commercial Seaports of Gdansk and Gdynia, and the Szczecin/Swinoujscie Port Group.

Such a concentration of port services, together with the high specialisation of both types and directions of cargoes and ships in Poland's ports, led to almost total monopolisation of the port services market typical of the state system of regulation, but disadvantageous from the point of view of the port services customers. This model eliminated every sign of competition in the sphere of the production of port services, which in turn did not favour organisational or technical advancement in the seaports. As a result, Poland's seaports preferred extensive, slow and very unambitious development, avoiding greater risks in either the operating or investment fields. This meant, however, that the technological and organisational distance between Polish ports and those of western Europe increased. This state of affairs was also strengthened by the fact that Poland's ports operated within a monopolistic transport and economic system and thus did not have to compete for Polish foreign trade cargoes. The flow of Polish, Czechoslovakian and Hungarian transit cargoes was determined for reasons other than those of a free economic market. This model of operation of Poland's ports was reflected negatively in their efficiency and output and in consequence upon their position on the international port services market.

The result of this system was that Poland's seaports were ill prepared to function under conditions of a market economy, in which the laws of competition are obligatory not only in external (international) but also internal (in the ports and the country) relations.

The new economic system assumes the firm's market control, based upon the principle of competitiveness and financial independence in respect of operational and investment activities, is carried out in an environment of progressive deregulation. This requires that Polish seaports undertake essential transformation of management systems, running parallel in the following three ways:

1.   in respect of subjective-proprietary relations, viz: organisational solutions in the administration of port land and water areas, including infrastructure;

2.   the seaport's management system which has a direct influence on the administration (i.e. maintenance, development and financing) of port infrastructure;

3.   structural changes in the organisation of operating activities, leading to the deconcentration of port services.

First and foremost, ownership relations in Poland's ports must be put in order, primarily in respect of port areas and the port infrastructure situated there. Ownership of the infrastructure is split between several subjects which conduct activities of different characters and are directed by their own economic interest, which constitutes the reason for the specific organisational disintegration of the ports. The administrators of the port areas are for example, port enterprises (Commercial Seaports in Gdansk and Gdynia and the Port Authority of Szczecin/Swinoujscie), ship yards and repair yards, sea fishery enterprises, service and industrial enterprises, etc.

In Poland, according to the law, some of the port areas constitute the property of the state, some of the town, and a small part - private property. These proportions are as follows:

Table 1
The share of particular forms of ownership of land areas in Polish seaports

Port	State ownership	Municipal ownership	Private ownership
Gdansk	90.6	9.1	0.3
Gdynia	97.3	1.1	1.6
Szczecin	71.4	28.6	-

Source: J.Doliwa-Dobrowolski: Projekt ustawy o portach morskich (Draft of the law on sea ports) Rzeczpospolita 12 March 1993

It can be seen that about 90% of the port land areas are currently the property of the state. Although their legal standing gives no rise to doubts, the authorities of the coastal towns claim rights to the port lands, considering themselves landlord of the areas upon which the seaports are situated.

Their use of port land areas can be presented with the example of the port of Szczecin/Swinoujscie.

Table 2
The users of port land areas in the framework of the forms of ownership occurring in the ports of Szczecin and Swinoujscie (%)

Users	Szczecin	Swinoujscie
Port Authority of Szczecin/Swinoujscie	47.8	21.0
Baltic Shipping Co.	-	2.0
Other enterprises located in the port	22.7	25.0
Szczecin Harbour Board	0.9	50.0
Town Council Board of Land Administration	28.6	-
Navy	-	2.0

Source: Assumptions to the project of the law on the maintaining of the seaports infrastructure (typescript) Gdansk 1991

The tenants administering port areas have the right of tenure derived from their existing presence there. In this situation, absence in Polish ports of a single tenant who would be owner of the whole port area, together with the infrastructure, and who would conduct rational management in respect of development and maintenance of technical potential, as well as managing the financial means available for this purpose, is a major drawback and has been recognised in the new laws on port ownership drawn up for Presidential acceptance in 1997/1998 and which will place the existing port authorities basically in the hands of the local city authorities and the State Treasury with, occasionally, some local, private input. Hopefully, this will avoid spatial conflicts arising between the city and port users, as well as other tenants operating in the port. Disputes in this respect are most frequently connected with land areas situated at the points of contact between port and city, or between individual users. The new structure will also facilitate the privatisation of port authorities sometime in the near future.

The structure of ownership formed in Poland's ports in the previous period is thus inadequate for the demands of a market economy and requires many basic changes. Arriving at one uniform opinion as to the future form of ownership structure in ports has been relatively difficult. There are numerous ideas as to who should manage the port areas and their infrastructure. It is here that the opinion of the state authorities, municipal authorities, employees, autonomous authorities and trade unions have conflicted and resulted in the slow progress that so far has been made towards reformation.

The drafts of the law on Polish seaports* drawn up in the early 1990s, constitute the starting point for defining the form of management of the country's seaports. All these drafts were unanimous as in recommending the introduction of principles of separating the sphere of management from operational activities, and the creation, for purposes of management of ports of central importance to the national economy (Gdansk, Gdynia and Szczecin/Swinoujscie), of "Port Authorities" as joint stock companies with the responsibility for public utilities. Divergences arise in the field of ownership, management (control) and utilisation of the port infrastructure. In this field the following options arose:

1.   The State Treasury, according to which the state will be willing to relinquish rights of ownership to land areas, to the extent to which their new owner (Port Authority - joint stock company or local authority) assumes the responsibility of co-financing the maintenance and development of the port infrastructure (from public funds of city authorities and intra port sources). Based on this assumption, the idea arose to establish port authorities as public utility joint stock companies, in which the State Treasury and territorial administrations would be (at least initially) the only shareholders (51% of the shares for the Treasury, at least 34% for the local authorities), and which would fulfill the duties of administrator in the ports.

2.   Municipal, demanding ownership of port land and that of the port infrastructure (apart from that of hydro-engineering), that is to say, withdrawal of the Treasury from ownership of port areas in favour of the local authorities. Management of seaports is of basic importance to the national economy and would rest in the hands of the port authorities as a public utility joint stock company directly connected with the port city.

3.   Ports with restricted autonomy, which would become owners of the port areas and their managers. They would be entitled to ownership of the land, buildings, appliances and equipment supplied by the Treasury and local authorities within the port boundaries. The administrative organ of the autonomic port would be the Autonomic Port Council, appointed by the Prime Minister and consisting of equal numbers of representatives of the territorial authorities and government administration.

* The following projects have been drawn up so far: The Ministry of Transport and Maritime Economy, the so-called Szczecin project, the Rotterdam group project drawn up on order of the World Bank, and two versions of the project of the Union of Maritime Towns and Parishes.

Regulating ownership relations was acknowledged to be of the first priority, as it constitutes the foundation for the new system of port management. According to the Act, land and port infrastructure contributed to the port authorities as joint stock companies by the Treasury and local authorities, become the property of the particular company. As a result of this, it will be possible to eliminate conflict between the Treasury and local authorities in respect of ownership.

In all drafts it is emphasised that port waters and objects of the hydro-engineering infrastructure, viz. fairways, channels, anchorages, manoeuvring basins, breakwaters, navigation markings and building structures ensuring access to the ports, constitute the property of the Treasury, and are excluded from turnover and as such cannot be included in the assets of the joint stock company which administers the port.

The activities of the joint stock company managing the port are to be:

1. forecasting, programming and planning of the port's development,
2. planning the spatial organisation of the port area,
3. obtaining new land for the spatial development of the port,
4. building, extending, maintaining and modernising the port infrastructure managed by the company, and particularly ensuring that it is maintained in a good technical-operational state of efficiency; the handling of investments and repairs, ensuring financial means to cover costs of maintenance, reconstruction and development,
5. management of land and port equipment (purchase, sale, leasing, renting) to ensure rational utilisation,
6. establishment of legal, economic and technical conditions to ensure appropriate functioning of the ports,
7. defining the principles and methods of utilising land, buildings, port appliances and equipment,
8. establishing and collecting general port dues including those for tonnage, berthing, passengers, cargo,
9. handling of port finances,
10. maintaining port fire precautions, salvaging and protection of port objects,
11. co-operation with government administration bodies operating in the port area,
12. port marketing and promotion,
13. representing the port in domestic and foreign relations,
14. initiating and financing of research for the needs of the port.

The founders of the company are to contribute capital stock in the shape of material contributions i.e. rights of ownership of port land and infrastructure.

The draft law on seaports which is expected to become law in late 1997 or 1998 anticipates the port authority becoming self financing and, thus, profitable. The sources of incomes of the port authority are derivatives of its status as owner of the port land and infrastructure. These are, in particular:

1. payments for permanent use and leasing of land situated within the port,
2. payments for lease or hire of port appliances and equipment,
3. general port dues i.e. tonnage, mooring, harbour, passenger and cargo dues,
4. income from the sale of port lands, buildings, equipment and appliances,
5. income from the supply of water, electrical power, dunnage.

Income earned by the port authorities will be allocated to the fulfilment of their statutory tasks i.e.- mainly the maintenance and development of the port infrastructure.

The drafts of the law indicate that the port authorities should be exempt from land tax and the reduction of income tax by a sum designed for the financing of the port infrastructure. The Treasury may award subventions for expenditure connected with the building and maintenance of port basins together with their hydro-engineering infrastructure.

As regards the remaining ports which are of no sizeable importance to the country's economy, the principles of their management are defined by the respective city authorities, when they have accepted ownership of port territories which previously constituted the property of the Treasury.

The port's water areas and technical infrastructure remain the property of the Treasury (similar to the case of the ports of primordial importance), which also remains responsible for their maintenance in proper technical-operational condition.

According to the proposed structure of port management, the economic-legal relationship between port authorities and enterprises offering port services are to depend on the relations between the lessors and lessees of port land areas or equipment. In this way, the port authorities' responsibilities will include the establishment and maintainance of the port's material-technical bases on which the operating enterprises (usually private) will be able to afford services to both ships and cargoes.

The coming into force of this law on ports and, in particular, the separation of the administrative tasks from those which are operational will create a new situation in Poland's seaports, reflecting the organisational and management structures that have been adopted in countries boasting market economies.

Along with the separation of the administration-management function from operating activities, the other stage in the change-over in seaports' administrative and operational activities and structure in Poland has been the handing over of operational activities to independent, private enterprises operating on commercial principles. In forming the operational ownership structure in seaports, attention has been paid to ensure that the new enterprises have at their disposal the necessary production potential, enabling them to survive in a free market of port services and development, and that the legal-economic relations between them and the port authorities facilitates the establishment and regulation of competition within the port.

Achieving the final form of organisation in the operating sphere in Poland's seaports will be a prolonged process, as is indicated by the transformation and state of organisational arrangements in the ports of Gdynia, Gdansk and Szczecin/Swinoujscie so far.

The privatisation of Polish shipping. Present situation and development

Janusz Zurek
Institute for Maritime Transport and Seaborne Trade
University of Gdansk

Abstract

This paper presents an analysis of the situation up to around the beginning of 1995 in the Polish shipping industry with respect to the privatisation process and in particular the events at the state liner operator, Polish Ocean Lines of Gdynia.

The state of the privatisation processes in Polish shipping enterprises

The main bases of Poland's economic reforms are changes of ownership, which should be treated as the leading element in the transformation of Poland's economy towards a market economy. These changes will enforce active adaptation on the part of economic structures and the market mechanism will enable the more effective allocation of resources by eliminating unremunerative structures and appropriate transfer of means to profit making enterprises.

Transformations of ownership are particularly important within the group of enterprises which operate on the line of contact with the international market. In the maritime sector, this concerns primarily, shipping and port enterprises, as well as smaller units connected with port-sea turnovers.

The necessity for the transformation has many origins which mainly stem from the international market, i.e. they must accept the laws and principles of operation characteristic of this market and adapt to the rules controlling the market mechanism. Apart from this, a change in form of ownership should improve the effectiveness of firms' operations making them credible thanks to the existence of an unequivocally defined owner, which is of particular importance in negotiations with foreign investors. It should be noted, however, that such transformation is relatively slow, mainly as a result of unfavourable conditions present in and around the enterprises themselves.

The main barrier in ownership transformation is the poor, and in some cases bad, financial position of companies, arising as a consequence of unfavourable trends characteristic of the world market, as well as the economic-political crisis and thus lack of stability in the Polish economy. Apart from this, shipowning enterprises display considerable susceptibility to fluctuations on the world market, which have a direct influence upon their activities. The huge capital located in the structure of assets of such enterprises and their absolute size also constitute an obstruction to the process of transformation. Large enterprises are less flexible to manage and are slower to react to changes in the market mechanisms. Apart from this, we still have to deal with the shortage of domestic capital, which means that the possibilities of encouraging its investment in the process of conversion of ownership of shipping enterprises is considerably restricted. Thus complete change in the ownership structure of enterprises usually requires both time and persistence.

The main barrier in the privatisation process of shipping enterprises is primarily their difficult economic-financial situation. Numerous factors contribute to this situation, some lying not only within the enterprises themselves, but also outside of them. The persistent recession on the world shipping market, primarily due to the substantial oversupply of tonnage (this in various tonnage sizes and types), has been exacerbated by the introduction of modern techniques and technologies, as well as efficient organisations in competing shipping companies around the world. Another factor influencing the freight market, is the relatively small increase in world seaborne turnover, out of proportion to the increase in carriage capacity offered. The financial situation of shipping enterprises is unfavourably influenced by rapidly increasing operating costs in Poland which are, to various degrees, the consequence of inflation. In effect, difficulties in the acquisition of cargo are increasing, resulting in fierce competition on the world's shipping market.

The most unpropitious of the external domestic conditions is the relatively slow rate of increase in production, which is due, to a certain degree, to the economic-organisational and technical conditions of the former economic system. Apart from this, the period of economic transformation towards a market economy had an unfavourable effect on the scale of production, causing a total change in the system of management and distinct change in structure of production. In consequence, there took place a substantial drop in Poland's seaborne trade turnover in the first half of the 1990s which is only now, in 1996/7, showing signs of real recovery and growth. A further drop was also noted in the carriage of transit cargoes, which together with Poland's foreign trade cargoes constituted a traditionally important back up for the Polish fleet.

This situation forces domestic owners to seek cargoes on the world shipping market, which, in view of the noncompetitive quality of service offered by the fleet, means that the cargoes gained for carriage are not often those highest paid.

Other local conditions which have had a negative influence on the situation of shipping enterprises include the persistently high level of inflation which influences costs, shipping firms being unable to shift such increases on to the carriage costs, and the restrictive financial and monetary-credit policies including the very high interest on credit which have severely inhibited investment processes.

The present state of shipowning enterprises is also the consequence of certain activities inherent in the enterprises themselves. Attention should be primarily paid (sometimes through no fault of the enterprises) to a lack of continuity in investment policy conducted over a longer period of time and also on such situations in which tonnage investments turned out to have misfired economically. Apart from this, self preservation steps were taken by some enterprises solely for the purpose of survival. Enterprises cannot be economically salvaged by the systematic sale of fixed assets i.e. the sale of means of production (unless they are worn out and technically out of date). This is more than likely to lead to self-annihilation, where there are no new tonnage investments to fill in the gaps. In this situation, of some significance to the enterprise is the use made of the financial gains from sales i.e. to what extent they are used to replenish the firm's funds, and to what extent such funds are used for consumption or repayment of debts? Another problem constitutes the frequently not too carefully considered operating decisions, which give rise to substantial increases in costs which are unjustified in many cases. There thus exists a need to discipline control of costs at the point of origin. In the case in point here, this concerns container operation to a considerable degree.

The maintainance of non-profitable lines, for an over extended period of time, thus giving rise to unnecessary increases in costs, is difficult to explain logically. Such a situation may, in time, cost an enterprise much more than the closing down of the service. Such lines should not and in fact cannot, be retained in a market economy, taking account only of any prestige benefits, or explaining the situation away with the excuse that the unfavourable situation is of a transitory character.

An unfavourable element affecting the present day financial situation of all shipowners' enterprises, is the maintainance of standby pools of crews, which constitute a serious financial burden. Crews should be taken from the market, which can be organised, for example, in the form of a specific 'Owners Crewing Agency' acting as intermediary in the signing on of crews.

Additional factors hindering financial crisis management include the continued attitude of employees towards their place of work as not being "their firm", particularly in respect of state owned enterprises; various types of internal conflicts, as well as an element of conservatism in the management system.

Just as important in improving efficiency of operations of shipping enterprises, are suitable organisational structures, which should help to guarantee efficiency and flexibility, as well as ensuring fast flow of information, to help improve the soundness of decision taking.

The effectiveness of any shipowning enterprise will also depend on the type of activities conducted. The holding on to and expansion of a narrow specialisation is unacceptable in the market conditions of today. The diversification of activities should be noted i.e. introduction into the firm's structure of various kinds and forms of activities which might support and supplement each other, or concentrate on additional and different forms.

Another perceptible barrier against increased effectiveness of operation is the size of the shipowning enterprise and related difficulties in its flexible and efficient management. The initial structure of Polish Ocean Lines (POL), operating liner tonnage, was multi-departmental and based on geographical route characteristics. These were organisational units without legal status and hence independent only to a certain degree. On 1 September 1986, POL was transformed into a uniform central organisation operating on the basis of an integrated structure.

Thus the operating departments were done away with and the firm's structure assumed a functional form. This decision was explained, among other things, by the unnecessary competition between departments that it created, noting only the unfavourable effects upon the company, instead of viewing competition as a stimulating factor acting as motivation for intensive activities. Treated in economic categories, competition generates initiative and progress, forces one to think and is thus in every respect a positive phenomenon.

Privatisation, the basic element of structural transformation, proceeds relatively slowly in shipping enterprises. Such a situation is mainly the result of the size of the enterprises, the immense value of their assets, the relatively poor financial situation of the operators, which in the case of POL is frankly bad, and too high a degree of investment risk given the present state of the freight market. Due to these factors, interest in changes in the structure of ownership is indeed modest on the part of domestic private capital, natural persons and foreign capital.

The process of privatisation of such large organisations as shipping enterprises in Poland, is primarily a question of putting their finances in order, improving the enterprise's management system and organisational structure, as well as the question of the existence and proper functioning of the capital market and freight market activity.

The solutions pertaining to structural transformation which have been gradually introduced into Polish Ocean Lines, are primarily concentrated upon the creation of a specific type of holding maintaining a hierarchy of economic authority between the so-called holding company (mother company) and dependent companies (daughter companies), in which the first control the subordinate daughter companies, through holding the controlling package of shares.

In the case of a holding structure as established in POL, the state owned (holding) company is the owner of state assets i.e. ships, containers, gearing, buildings, and also owns shares in the daughter (or filial) companies, simultaneously leasing them productive and non-productive assets.

This is not, however, a solution which is suitable for new filial companies initially because of the considerable burden of costs which the holding company are likely to place upon them. These companies dependent upon the holding company, will find that without access to a share of their own or outside capital their position in the market will be weak. Thus to strengthen the position of these companies, there needs to be the backing of Polish and other capital and it is essential that it should be organised upon a commercial basis.

In a legal sense, subordinate companies constitute separate, individual economic units, connected and controlled by means of capital to the mother company, which owns the main share of the assets. Daughter companies, as operating companies, have their own management as well as choice of field and subject of operation. They must cover commitments arising in consequence of their activities.

The creation of the holding company structure in POL is primarily:

-to improve economic effectiveness of the company,
-ensure efficient administration and management of finances,
-to keep pace with the increasing competition, by more flexible and active market operations,
-to improve operational decision-making,
-to increase the chances of attracting foreign capital interested in participating in the enterprise,
-to enable the free transfer of profits between companies, and thus create potential conditions which minimise the tax burden,
-to heighten the interest of management and employees in the financial effects and distribution of income.

The first company to become part of POL's holding, was established on 1 September 1991, based upon the Szczecin branch of the firm, under the name "Euroafrica". This company operates using tonnage leased from POL and other owners. POL have shares in the company. The majority of the shares belong to private persons and firms, these amounting to over 50%, thus enabling the change in the company's status to become a private company.

The company's tonnage operates mainly on short range runs i.e. the UK, Scandinavia, western Europe, and some rather more distant services to west Africa. Euroafrica is the first example of privatisation of state owned shipping enterprises in Poland. The impact upon the company's activities so far, indicates that the undertaking has been effective and confirms the argument for the need for further such steps.

"Pol-Levant Shipping Lines", operating ships leased from POL, opened their doors in May 1993 with the Mediterranean routes of the old company . Alongside POL, Euroafrica, was also a partner, owning the greatest number of shares, thus changing the ownership structure and making Pol-Levant a private company.

As from 1 June 1993, "Pol-America Joint Stock Company" (formerly Polish Shipping Association) began operating as a shipowner, utilising its own tonnage and that chartered from POL, employed on the South American route. Shareholders in the company are Euroafrica and Pol-Levant Shipping Lines. The company at present operates on three of POL's South American Lines: to the west and east coast of South America and the Caribbean Line.

A number of other subsidiaries have been created by 1997 so that some 14 daughter companies now exist covering crew supply, the Asian routes, port and ships agency work and the North American routes amongst others. These companies are now beginning to extend their activities beyond their original definition to cover new markets and opportunities.

Included in these operating companies, three in particular can be noted. The first, established on 1 July 1992 as POLCONTAINER Agency Company, is engaged in operating containers and container equipment, as well as organising container turnover in the hinterland, in the name, and on account of POL. The company operates on the basis of an agency agreement signed with POL.

POL owns 49% of the shares in the company. Apart from work for POL's operating services, the company also carries out work for foreign customers.

On 1 January 1993, the second company commenced operating, i.e. the transport-forwarding-agency company of "Franck and Tobiesen Poland Ltd., Shipping and Forwarding" engaged in the operating of overland transport means leased from POL as well as forwarding and brokerage services. The major part of the company's shares - 51% of the founder's capital, is in the hands of the Danes, whereas POL have 49%.

"POL Supply Ltd" was founded on the basis of POL's Supply and Transport Department. This is a limited liability company with some German capital. The company will manage POL's assets in their name, the range of activities including trade, transport, forwarding, ship-chandling, warehouse facilities, etc.

The holding concept should accelerate the process of privatisation with these smaller organisations, and although with less capital at their disposal, they are operationally more efficient and can keep a careful check on costs essential to achieving satisfactory financial results. Given these conditions, they may become the subject of interest of domestic and foreign natural and legal persons, as well as other, already privatised companies of POL, or the company employees themselves.

Finally, the process of structural transformation within POL, should lead to the transformation of POL itself - acting as a holding company and currently still a state owned enterprise on the strength of the decision of the Ministry of Transport and Maritime Economy - into a joint stock company with the state as the sole shareholder, with all legal consequences and opportunities that might result from this.

Proposals for further privatisation in shipping enterprises

Since 1991, POL has been entering a succession of stages of structural transformation. The specific type of holding company that Polish Ocean Lines state owned enterprise has become and to which filial companies are subordinated as regards capital, does not create suitable conditions for the development and creation of new and additional capital in such companies. As a result of their direct connections with the mother company, these companies are obliged to transmit considerable sums as rent e.g. for accommodation, and thus gradually repay POL's debts. The amount of these payments to the mother company, encourages the retention of undeveloped and to a large extent, ineffective management structures. These structures have changed very little in operational principle and the holding administration remains far too big, continuing with a highly centralised structure. This clearly restricts the developmental possibilities of the new offshoots from POL.

In which direction should steps be taken? POL continues to be subordinate to the Ministry of Transport and Maritime Economy and more recently in 1996, the Treasury. The latter, having in mind acceleration of the process of privatisation, considered a solution which would open the way for changes in the structure of ownership and facilitate the process of privatisation. This was to establish several separate shipping enterprises of legal entity as wholly independent units. These enterprises would be separated depending upon their geographical directions, similar to the former multi-departmental enterprises, but the difference being of course, that these former groupings did not have any legal status.

These enterprises, which would have at their disposal tonnage of specific technical-operational parameters, would, in time, become joint stock companies with the state as the sole shareholder. The value of the assets of these companies would be much smaller, thus facilitating the privatisation process.

Breaking down enterprises into several smaller ones, will improve the efficiency of operation, simplify management, smooth out noticeably the organisational structure and in effect, improve the economic results (a good example of this is the Pol-Levant filial company). These newly established enterprises, bound by specific contracts, were committed to gradual repayment of debt, thus helping to solve what would otherwise be an impossible task for POL.

What alternative arrangement of enterprises could be suggested? Having in mind the geographic-functional criteria, one could consider one enterprise concentrating on servicing the North, South and Central American routes (to a certain extent, Pol-America filial company fits this). A second enterprise would cover the Asia and Australia runs. The third - the Mediterranean Line (to a certain extent Pol-Levant Co Ltd would be suitable) could cover the ports in that basin. A fourth enterprise (with its seat in Szczecin) could operate on the African routes.

One way of privatising, in view of the still substantial assets, would be to convert these enterprises into joint stock companies with the state as sole shareholder. In this way, much better conditions for placing enterprises on the market would be created, this in turn, helping to improve their economic results. Such enterprises would also have a better possibility of co-operating with foreign capital, which would be highly desirable, if only to improve the enterprise's image in the marketplace. The strengthening of the position of these enterprises in the market and thus improving their financial standing would create favourable conditions for preparing for the issue of shares, in which both Polish and foreign capital might be interested, as well as a percentage of staff (i.e. natural persons from Poland). In this way the given enterprise would be on its way to capital privatisation which, in the light of the improvement of its efficiency, may attract the interest of both domestic and foreign capital.

Another advantageous privatisation solution could also be the choice of another form, namely the payment for stock/shares in instalments. This form of privatisation, leading to the purchase of a specific enterprise in instalments, has the advantage, that ownership would be immediately transferred to the purchaser, affording him the possibility of managing the firm and utilising its potential. Apart from this, given the present state of capital resources on the domestic market, this form can be introduced immediately. Adopting this method of privatisation, the sale of stocks/shares takes place on credit terms, but ones which are realistic and which are accepted by the market.

Finally, just a few words on the other two major state ship operators in Poland. The privatisation of Poland's second shipowner - Polish Steamship Company (PZB), has so far, been conducted slightly differently. This firm is considering the concept of actively using the Polish Shipping Joint Stock Company (ZPSA) in the privatisation process, which is in fact the owner of a large number of the vessels operated by Polish Steamship Co. This company will constitute the starting point for preparing for further stages in the privatisation process.

The possibility of accepting a similar manner of privatisation to that proposed in the case of POL has been considered and in view of the size of Polish Steamship Co, the breakdown of the firm into smaller organisational units more suitable for privatisation, has commenced. Guided mainly by functional criteria, a tramping enterprise has been established in Szczecin (Polsteam Shortramp); this specialises in the carriage of dry bulk cargoes and the operation of ships with a tonnage not exceeding 15,000 tons, which are able to sail up to the port of Szczecin. A second tramping enterprise with its seat at Swinoujscie (Polsteam Oceantramp), employs ships with tonnages not exceeding 65-70,000 tons, which are able to call at that port. The third tramping enterprise is located at Gdynia and operates tankers (Polsteam Tankers), mainly for the carriage of crude oil and its products and liquid sulphur.

Poland's third shipowner as regards size is Polish Baltic Shipping Co. of Kolobrzeg (PZB). It was the only one to undergo conversion into a joint stock company with the state as the sole shareholder and as from that moment has been subordinate to the Ministry of Privatisation (now, 1997, the Treasury) and subject to the rules connected with this method of privatisation. At this point, a problem which is difficult to solve appears, namely the assessment of the assets, which are much more extensive than in the case of the previously mentioned enterprises (mainly concerning the land of the port of Kolobrzeg and the ferry terminal at Swinoujscie). Another question that will have to be addressed before privatisation can really progress is that of improving the financial situation of the enterprise, which is currently very poor and clearly very important from the point of view of its market value and appeal.

Polish shipping under market conditions

Maciej Krzyzanowski and E. Skurewicz
Maritime Institute, Gdansk

Abstract

This paper provides a short review of the Polish shipping market at a time of major transformation.

Introduction

The programme of fundamental economic and social reforms in Poland which began at the end of 1989 was formulated in close co-operation with the International Monetary Fund (IMF). The government that was implementing the programme, introduced a set of emergency measures in order to arrest the deterioration of the economy of the country and to establish foundations for the comprehensive adjustment programme in 1990.

The formulated measures included the following steps:

-In order to curb wage inflation a tax on wage increases that exceeded 80% of monthly rise of cost of living index.

-Accelerated tax payments and cuts in budget expenditures, mostly subsidies, helped to reduce the budget deficit from 10% to 7% of GDP.

-In preparating the ground for price liberalisation, many price controls were lifted.

-To curb excessive money creation, intensified credit restraint was implemented.

-To narrow the spread between the official rate and rates in parallel markets, accelerated depreciation of the official exchange rate was introduced, establishing the foundation for the introduction of internal convertibility of the Polish currency (initially US$ = 9,500 Zloty).

The intention was to balance the supply and demand for foreign exchange and to unify a segmented foreign exchange market.

Despite these measures the economy remained depressed. Industrial output was declining and food shortages intensified. Farmers hoarded their products in anticipation of further inflation.

In order to improve the economic situation of the country, a stabilisation programme was introduced, prepared by a team of Polish economists led by the Deputy Prime Minister Leszek Bacerowicz in close collaboration with international experts - mostly IMF consultants.

Deep cuts in government expenditure, drastic restrictions imposed upon credit creation and money supply through rising interest rates, a sharp devaluation of the Polish zloty, and a restrictive incomes policy, had a very positive economic impact by the end of the year. Rampant inflation was stopped, currency stabilised, the internal market boomed and foreign trade relations, especially in exports, substantially improved. The shipping companies operating in crosstrades achieved considerable profits, mostly as a result of the favourable exchange rate.

In spite of these achievements, the whole economic system of the country was still in crisis. On the positive side, however, was the unprecedented readiness of the people to accept radical and difficult measures and to support the new government in overcoming the crisis. The strategic objective of the government was to establish an open market economy system in Poland, relying on a strong private sector and guided by profit motives. The government started with the following broad initiatives:

-foreign sector liberalisation;
-large scale privatisation of the state-sector of the economy;
-introduction of market economy related institutions and mechanisms.

Trade and shipping reforms

The reforms in trade so far, have eliminated remaining elements of the state monopoly and allowed for virtually unrestricted access to foreign trade activities for all economic organisations. Also, all quantitative restrictions have been lifted on imports and only a few remain for exports.

Foreign trade liberalisation was accompanied by corresponding liberalisation of the foreign exchange system and administrative allocation of foreign currencies was also ended. The ambitious task of transforming the Polish economy from a centrally planned system to a market economy within a few years was probably more difficult than the implementation of the stabilisation programme.

No country has ever undertaken this kind of transformation, so there is no precedent on which to draw. Also, the theory concerning this type of transformation is still to be formulated.

The rules of the new economic market oriented policy recently introduced by the government are stimulating shipping companies to undertake modernisation programmes in the face of increased competition within the different shipping spot markets. The growing shippers' demands have to be reflected in an improvement in the quality of shipping services at least in part by following trends set by new transport technologies.

Also, modern methods of organisation are indispensable for effecting better utilisation of the existing potential of the fleet, increasing ship productivity, lowering the cost of operation and thus preparing the industry to face the new market demands and the rigid conditions which stem from the financial reforms introduced progressively through the 1990s.

To complicate matters, in general, cargo vessels have to meet world standards with regard to technical design, cargo transport technology, cargo gear, navigation and communication equipment, energy saving propulsion and with regards to environmental protection systems, degree of automation and computerisation. These demands have now to be faced by the Polish shipping industry at a time when there are increasingly sizeable financial demands placed upon the sector and little room for economic manoeuvring.

The present phase of the reconstruction of the Polish commercial fleet can be defined as an adaptation process to the new conditions of the market economy and optimisation of the fleet's size and the characteristics of the ship's technical and technological parameters.

As the main factors influencing this process, the following can be recognised:

-a decrease of the volume of Polish international trade and transit in Polish ports;
-the new government financial policy; in particular stabilisation of the exchange rate of the Polish zloty with the aim of achieving a convertible currency;
-the necessity of replacement and modernisation of ships now in operation.

Analysis of statistical data on the initial phase of change in the Polish fleet from 1988-1990 shows that the number of ships and total deadweight are decreasing. The number of ships was 23 units less, corresponding to a 9.3% decrease, whilst the deadweight capacity had declined by around 94,600 tonnes, corresponding to a 2.4% decrease.

Simultaneously, the increase in the average tonnage of ships was observed to rise from 15,900 tonnes in 1988 to 17,100 tonnes in 1990, while the average index decreased at that time.

The process of the progressive decrease of number of ships of the Polish fleet does not mean that their carrying capacity had decreased. As a result of tonnage modernisation and new ships entering service, the average unit carrying capacity increased. The Polish fleet in 1988 transported 30,263,000 tonnes of cargo and in 1990 28,477,000 tonnes - a 9.2% decrease.

The main characteristic feature was the increase of foreign cargo share in Polish fleet shipping. In 1988 it amounted to 33.7%, increasing to 48.9% in 1990. Simultaneously the decrease in share of the Polish fleet of Polish foreign trade by sea should be noted. In 1988 it amounted to 48.7% and decreased to 38.9% in 1990. These data indicate that the Polish fleet increased its participation in the international shipping market following the social, political and economic changes of the late 1980s.

Finally we can conclude here that the doctrine of Polish fleet development in force, until recently based upon a predominance of domestic foreign trade needs, is losing its significance. The basic reasons for this phenomenon are:

-implementation of market principles in shipping companies and foreign trade enterprises;
-changes in seaborne Polish foreign trade in reference to volume, balance of imports and exports and diversification of goods;
-optimisation of economic transformation for Polish carriers, shipowners and foreign trade enterprises.

Poland in the Southern Baltic transit market

Krystyna Wasilewska
Institute of Maritime Transport and Seaborne Trade
University of Gdansk

Abstract

This paper examines the role of Polish ports and shipping as part of the Trans European Motorway system linking many of the countries of eastern and southern Europe with those of Scandinavia. The significant issues that stem from this transit role for the maritime sector are discussed in the light of changing economic pressures and market demands.

Introduction

Since the founding of the Council for Mutual Economic Assistance (CMEA), the co-incidence of the shipping and inland transport modes at the port interface has been treated in Poland as an element of national economic policy. Although the ports sector brought several economic benefits, it was also a source of serious problems, especially before the modernisation of Polish seaports which took place between the sixties and seventies. Problems arose from the lack of handling capacity - insufficient even for handling Polish foreign trade. Moreover, rouble clearing schemes made the whole transit process unprofitable with respect to service provision and as a consequence, no investment occurred directed towards transit cargoes. Such cargoes were treated as supplementary to the main cargo, even though every decrease in their volume caused concern because it indirectly indicated a worsening of the competitive situation of Polish seaports and of Polish commodities.

Political and economic changes in central and eastern Europe have caused the following:

-probably a permanent loss of transit hinterland situated to the south and west of former Czechoslovakia;

-temporary breakdown in transit through the Polish ports, regarding Czech and Slovak cargoes;

-opening of a potential hinterland embracing the territory of the former USSR countries. The capture of this market would create possibilities for entering other fragmentary markets (e.g. investment markets) in new countries;

-new competitors on the south Baltic transit market (such as ports of the former GDR and Soviet Union).

Attempts to analyse new transit markets in central and eastern Europe commonly concentrate on the direction of trade of the cargo movements, and rarely mention the cargo structure. This is as a result of the following:

-the southern Baltic transit market is only just being developed;

-there is a lack of sufficient data to forecast the direction and rate of economic development in new countries which constitute a potential transit hinterland for the Baltic countries.

Factors determining the south Baltic transit markets in the nineties

In the nineties, the transit market in the Baltic Sea region is being formed not only by the network of transport routes developed in the last decade - determined by such hinterland elements as the price of transport and port services, but also, to a greater degree by the factors which affect the prosperity and potential of the port's foreland.

A serious decline in maritime trade of the members of the former CMEA has resulted in a decrease of these Baltic ports' turnover and as a consequence, this has diminished port competitiveness. The decline in port turnover is followed by a reduction of regular lines and sailing frequencies and hence the attractiveness of the port for general cargo in transit continues to diminish. The drop in turnover has also caused a surplus of handling capacity over existing demand, thus effecting a setback in investment, which results in ageing of the technical potential of the port.

All these factors have occurred in Polish seaports, reducing transit cargoes to those which are less sensitive to the above mentioned developments. A breakdown of transit through Polish seaports at the beginning of the nineties resulted from changes in direction and structure of foreign trade of the CMEA members. Traditional partners from overseas including many developing countries, were totally eliminated from the foreign trade of central and eastern European countries. Newly established small trade enterprises import commodities through western European firms, mostly German. In that way, transhipment through Polish ports was eliminated in favour of land transportation. Highly developed countries are dominating among the present foreign contracting parties. In the general cargo case, they support mostly containerised commodities. Regarding trans-oceanic container transportation, Polish seaports are uncompetitive in their local international hinterland (i.e. central European countries) - mostly due to the lack of specialised regular lines which once existed in the past, but which have now been transferred to the ports of the North Sea. Transfer of the base ports for transoceanic container lines into peripheral regions does not depend upon largely internal Polish factors - and with a view to Polish transit policy and prospects, it must be treated as a permanent move.

When evaluating the competitiveness of Polish seaports in terms of the present pattern of cargo movement, it can be stated that the level of services for almost all cargo groups is similar to other south Baltic ports. In the southern Baltic transit market one may include: Kiel, Travemunde, Lubeck, Wismar, Rostock, Straslund, Sassnitz/Mukran, Kaliningrad, Klaipeda, Lipawa, Windawa, Riga, Parnawa, Tallinn/Muuga, St Petersburg and a number of new Russian ports which are projected. Nearly all these ports are implementing or constructing development plans to improve their competitive positions on the southern Baltic market. Moreover, Russia has decided to build three new ports on the Baltic: Primorsk on the Northern coast of the Finnish Gulf (oil, petroleum products, liquid gas), Buchta Batarejnana - on the southern Coast of the Finnish Gulf (petroleum products) and Ust-Luga (dry bulk and containers). The overall project has been accepted by a government commission as an integral part of a large programme which is to be realised under the President's edict.

Changes in direction and intensity of cargo movements at the beginning of the nineties have made officials, who exercised control over transit services' supply, to elaborate development plans not only for the ports but also for hinterland transport and shipping (ferry shipping mostly) - as they expect the cargo supply to increase substantially.

The organisations with interests in foreign trade in countries of this region are developing a variety of multivariate expansion plans - often rather hazy in the case of post-socialist countries, but clearly viable in the case of the Scandinavian countries. In Sweden and Finland, which constitute the most important Scandinavian foreland for Polish ports, the many variants that exist are caused by a lack of conviction regarding the direction and intensity of the economic integration that is expected to occur.

Swedish economic groups in particular, present different standpoints when forecasting the direction of national trade expansion. The present political and economic changes in Europe are encouraging Swedish hopes for new markets very soon. An economic lobby, which developed before Sweden entered the European Union in 1995, expects the biggest opportunities for Swedish economic expansion to be the West European markets which had been previously separated from EFTA countries by tariff walls.

A lobby directed towards quite new markets promotes expansion to the eastern European countries, including Russia. There is still a lack of sufficient data to forecast a rapid growth in Swedish turnover with Ukraine, Belorussia or the former Baltic Republics. Possibilities of development in trade between Sweden and Poland are more easily justified. Meanwhile, Swedish studies still suggest that one day at least some countries in that region will become viable consumption markets and thus will turn out to be to the exporters' advantage (those who manage to reorient towards those markets on time) (1). Hence, the Swedish are preparing very carefully for trade development in south-eastern directions.

There are also complex arrangements which embrace not only the former CMEA countries, but also the Far East and Near East - as an expansion area through the Baltic Sea and beyond by land transportation. It should be noted, that the success of all these Scandinavian plans may radically transform the south Baltic transit market.

Meanwhile, Swedish preparations for the European Union and the west European market includes the completion of a new, permanent rail-road connection between Germany and Sweden (via Denmark). Connection through the Store Belt of 18km length is expected to be open for rail transport in 1997, and for road transport in 1998. It is also planned to construct other permanent connections through Oresund. Swedish investments in the western direction will comprise (beside participation in fixed connections through Denmark) building fast ferries (45 knots) destined for operation on the lines leading to Holland and France. Duration of voyage between Gothenburg and Zeebruge is expected to be reduced from 36 to 12 hours. This last plan was developed as a consequence of the congestion on German roads, which has also influenced the development of transit connections through Poland.

Regarding southern and eastern directions, Sweden is planning to extend the road network between 1994-2003 at a cost of 45 billion krones. Road investment is mostly directed towards the eastern ports, with an expected growth in ferry transportation to Poland and the FSU and from links with the Trans-Siberian railway line and with the Trans-European North-South Motorway (TEM).

Projects for the Scandinavian part of the TEM are already being prepared. A motorway beginning in Oslo will run via Gothenburg, Borls and Vaxjo to Karlskrona (2). The Swedish project includes utilisation of the ferry line between Karlskrone and Gdynia which is thought to be the most favourable to incorporate Sweden effectively into the TEM.

For Sweden, the TEM provides not only access to the Czech, Slovak and Hungarian markets but also to southern European and Near East countries - the trade with those countries is currently carried out by direct sea rather than ferry connections. The project to construct a Scandinavian part of the TEM corresponds with the ideas put forward by Sweden, Poland and Norway, who created a group called "Swe-No-Po". This group is preparing a project for a road-sea connection between Sweden, Norway and the Mediterranean Sea - through the TEM, the ferry connection between Karlskrona and Gdynia, ferry lines on the Mediterranean Sea and the Persian Gulf (3). It is expected that the duration of transportation between Norway and the Persian Gulf ports can be reduced form 14 to 4 days after completion of the TEM. The majority of destination points situated in the eastern part of the European coast of the Mediterranean Sea are located within reach of land transportation which does not exceed 48 hours - in comparison with a 10 day maritime voyage around western Europe.

Also, in the case of railways, Swedish projects are related to the Gdansk-Warsaw-Katowice arterial railway (TER). These projects are very advantageous in respect of the development of transit through Polish ports. Swedish projects dealing with the TEM and TER are assuming a serious share of total combined transport through Poland. It is undoubtedly a worthwhile exercise, as according to the "Swe-No-Po" group's estimate, at least 40% of turnover between Sweden/Norway and the Persian Gulf countries will be transported via the TEM and TER.

One issue of great importance from the point of view of Polish ports and their interests in the Scandinavian foreland, stems from the changes in location of reloading places for general cargo in transit. This development is particularly connected with the on-going transfer of handling places from conventional/general cargo regions and container bases to ferry terminals.

Projected demand for transit services in Polish seaports

The southern Baltic market for port transit services, which has developed due to the political and economic changes that have occurred in the region, can be assessed in three groups - southern, eastern and western.

In the present situation in the transit market, two groups are visible in the southern region - Poland and Germany. Cargoes appearing on that market embrace commodities from the Czech Republic, Slovakia, Hungary and Austria. Maritime trade of the first three of these countries has diminished in recent years. At the same time, changes in direction of maritime trade have caused a drop in the Polish share in handling the transit of these countries. For instance, at the beginning of the nineties, trade with China, highly significant in earlier years, almost stopped. In addition to this, a serious decline in transit in Polish ports in 1991 was caused by additional factors resulting from weak marketing during the rapid political change and liberalisation of the economy.

Polish ports are not attractive for Hungarian cargoes due to transportation costs, expressed both in time and transport distance. Without transformation of the whole logistical system and without large infrastructure investment, Hungarian transit will appear in Polish ports only in the case of a change in direction of Hungarian trade towards Scandinavia. The same situation exists when assessing possibilities of increasing present volumes in transit from the Czech Republic and Slovakia.

For the present, the prognosis of further development of trade turnover between the Czech Republic, Slovakia, Hungary, Austria and the Scandinavian countries is difficult to support. According to Swedish estimates, the Czech and Slovak share could rise to half of the present Finnish share by the turn of the century. This requires a growth of 15 times in comparison with the present state (taking into account the general growth of Swedish trade exchange). It will depend largely upon Polish determination whether Polish seaports will handle the increasing turnover of the Czech Republic and Slovakia with Norway and Sweden in a better proportion than at present.

Hungarian turnover with Sweden is now 25% lower than the aggregated turnovers of the Czech Republic and Slovakia. A small share of Polish ports in handling Hungarian cargoes supports the prognosis which assumes a serious rise in turnover only after removing the existing barriers.

In Austria's case, a significant growth in turnover is likely to occur due to the expected increase of Austrian-Swedish trade exchange (connected with the access of both countries to the European Union).

While analysing the cargo structure in North-South trade exchange, it is worthy of note that two thirds of Swedish exports by value to the Czech Republic and Slovakia are composed of transport components while the remainder is dominated by machinery and other equipment. Imports are made up of metallurgic articles, machines and furniture (4). Swedish exports to Hungary are dominated by paper, machines, telecommunication equipment and transport components, whilst meat, vegetables, fruits, metals and clothes dominate the imports.

In the field of transit services in Polish seaports in an eastbound direction, Poland handles maritime trade for Belorussia, Russia and Ukraine. Countries established after the USSR collapse, soon attempted to become partners within the process of international economic cooperation. However, whilst following this pattern, Belorussia and to some degree the Ukraine, were unable to break all economic relations with Russia - relying more on the existing and traditional economic relations than developing new ones.

According to data presented by 'The Russian Institute of the Commercial Fleet', Russian maritime cargo turnover amounts to 260 million tonnes each year, with transhipments in the northwest region accounting for 33% (5). Short term forecasts, which include the prospect of overcoming the present shortage of handling capacity in Russian ports, expect the turnover in the Baltic region to reach 148 million tonnes and as a consequence, transit through Polish ports should not only still be possible but should develop and expand. However, the structure of cargo is less easy to assess and because of the present economic problems, Russian imports and exports are highly unpredictable. Meanwhile Polish-Russian cooperation in transit requires detailed arrangements stemming from the types of cargoes that have to be considered. Oil exported by pipeline from Russia to the Northern Port in Gdansk is one rare example of a secured cargo, especially up until the construction of an alternative oil port in Primorsk.

As a consequence of its location, the Ukraine exports and imports through Polish territory, mainly in trade with Scandinavia. A quite different situation occurs with deep-sea trades, which can be served by the Ukrainian Black Sea ports. A similar situation occurs with west European relations which could be served by land transport or by the Black Sea ports. Meanwhile, trade exchange between Ukraine and Sweden/Norway is not yet well developed (6). Trade turnover with overseas countries through Polish seaports is also limited.

On the other hand, Belorussia may become an important transit partner if it develops maritime transport affiliated trades. Fertilisers, in which Belorussia specialised for the USSR, provide the country with its biggest opportunities. At present, the FSU does not take all Belorussian surplus production. Meanwhile, the world market for fertilisers has recently declined with the return of organic and natural farming methods, especially in the higher developed countries and consequently, there may be some problems in finding overseas markets for these products.

The total annual supply of basic Belorussian cargoes in transit through Polish seaports is estimated to reach 7-9million tonnes (7), of which general cargo (conventional and containerised) could amount to 30%. In the field of exports, such products as fertilisers, cement and oil products will be dominant; in imports major positions will be held by oil, aluminium, sugar, grain and rubber.

Serious transit activity in Polish ports in an eastbound direction will be realised only by lowering railway tariffs and changing certain customs regulations. Polish seaports could also gain additional transit cargo in the course of establishing free zones which will act also as distribution centres, and through concluding an agreement with Russia on coordination of port investment.

Investment activities are already underway, directed towards eastbound transit. A grain terminal in the North Port of Gdansk will soon be completed. Construction of a fertiliser terminal in the port of Gdansk, temporarily limited to cargo handling for import and export to and from Poland, will be continued only if Belorussia obtains large export contracts. Poland also offers port facilities for handling Belorussian tractors for export. Similar investment for handling Russian trade depend on mutual agreements.

All eastern regions provide greater supply of transit cargoes than the southern regions, but the latter tend to be dominated by general cargo whilst bulk cargo dominates in the eastern regions.

In recent years substantial growth has been observed in western regions, and hence Germany has grown as a special transit partner for Poland. Though a large part of Polish cargoes passes through German ports, some German cargoes are still handled in Polish ports. Many possibilities exist in the choice of transportation routes for Germany, causing instability in the structure and quantity of cargo that exists (as in the Russian case). Transit cargo is very diverse and includes in particular, oil transmitted by pipeline from Gdansk (the Northern port) to Schwedt and Leuna. The second cargo group which is being actively pursued, constitutes building materials and aggregates - required for the large restructuring investments underway in eastern Germany.

Serious investment in the Berlin region requires large supplies of these materials. With a view to those needs, traffic capacity of the German railways in a northern direction is almost totally utilised. The railway distance between Berlin and Rostock is some 250km and Berlin and Hamburg, 300km. This compares with the distance from Szczecin to Berlin and the import of these commodities through Poland is thus just a question of reducing transport costs.

Building materials and aggregates which might comprise a large proportion of maritime imports for the Berlin region, show a high affinity to inland water transportation. In this case, the distance between Berlin and Szczecin amounts to only 180km, and yet from Hamburg to Berlin, 360km. However, the worsening navigational situation on the Odra River has encouraged the German authorities to build Uckermunde port (to the south west of Swinoujscie) which since 1993, has handled transhipments to and from Berlin.

An increasing turnover of general cargo (also containerised) could be a further essential factor of growth in transit turnover with the west. The Via Hanseatica motorway construction project, running from Lubeck to the Polish border includes (as additional investment) the construction of large freight terminals in Lubeck, Rostock, Szczecin and Swinoujscie. Those investments will be operating in two ways: they will attract Polish commodities to German ports, but on the other hand they will attract German and other EU cargoes to the Szczecin-Swinoujscie port complex. In general, in spite of growing transit trades, they may well cause a decrease in turnover of Polish seaports.

Conclusions

While aiming at the long-term development of transit cargo movements in Polish ports, one must not forget to develop the logistical and industrial functions with additional customs free solutions to enhance clearance facilities. These facilities can be found in all major transit ports around the world in the form of duty free zones, which enable control to be retained over cargo without passing through expensive customs procedures (8).

Due to the differing types of cargo, these zones should be established for both ports and for distribution centres separately, with transhipment storage facilities. The latter should be established inside the port areas - the former in the port's neighbourhood. Both the ports in Szczecin-Swinoujscie and in Gdansk have at their disposal territory suitable for duty free zones and plans for their development as duty free zones.

Polish maritime ports are especially suited for establishing distribution and industrial centres directed towards the new east European markets. Industrial plants located there may also export their production to the Czech Republic, Hungary or Estonia. Weak capital resources in some countries in the region can be joined with foreign capital thus providing the chance to make export promoting investments in Polish ports.

Also, agreements with eastern neighbours of Poland concerning mutual transport investments could increase the competitiveness of Polish ports, for example by linking Gdynia and Gdansk by a new broad gauge railway line.

Nowadays, Poland faces the necessity for serious modernisation of the transport networks. According to a series of international agreements, this modernisation process will soon be carried out. All agreements referring to the TER , TEM and intermodal transport provide for improved international transport links and they are expected to satisfy the needs of transit movements through Poland. Moreover, the concentration of cargo passing between the Baltic ports and the countries of central/southern Europe and the Near East countries in the TEM/TER corridor could attract sizeable capital investment thus ensuring high quality improvements.

These activities will seriously influence the growth of transit turnover in Polish seaports and their realisation will improve the Polish position on the international transit market.

References

1   L. Por, O. Rask, L .Foberg, L. Enarson and P. Jannson (1993) 'Baltic
        Links - Potential for Trade and Transport across the South Baltic Sea'
        Institute for Transport Economics and Logistics, Hogskolan i Vaxjo,
        Sweden.

2   Pre-feasibility study 1993 Trans European Motorway Link Oslo-Warsaw/
        Lodz. TEM SCANDINAVIA Transek, Solna.

3   Shipping Lines on the Baltic and the North South Trans European
        Motorway. Inzynieria Morska i Geotechnika, no.3 p138.

4   Ibidem p51.

5   M. Krzyzanowski   (1994)   The Second Conference of Transport
        Ministries in the Baltic Countries, BoiGM, May p20.

6   Baltic Links p50.

7   E. Czuchnowska and M. Sloianko-Wasilewska (1993) 'Possibilities of
        handling Belorussian Cargoes by Polish sea transport' in 'Economic and
        legal changes in the Polish maritime economy'. International Scientific
        Conference, Gdansk 13-14 September, Maritime Institute, Gdansk.

8   A first step in that field may involve establishing a special economic zone
        - WOC, in Swinoujscie, which has been under the control of the Odra-
        Port company since June 1995.

The influence of changes in East European countries upon their merchant fleets

Tadeusz Lodykowski
Institute of Maritime Transport and Seaborne Trade
University of Gdansk

Abstract

This paper presents a longitudinal study of the changes which have taken place in the east European shipping industry, developing the theme from activities and events in the past, through the current phase with a look at the factors and issues that will be important in the future.

Introductory remarks

The changes which have taken place from the turn of the 1980s and 1990s in eastern Europe are undoubtedly the beginning of social, political and economic processes which will last for many years. The basic aim of these processes in the economic sphere, is the transition from a centralised economy, based on a form of state ownership, to a market economy under predominantly private ownership. The scale of problems faced is as large as the effects of the 70 years of the economic and social-political system which functioned in the east European countries.

The fundamental theme of these changes is, generally speaking, quite clear. It stems from the inefficiency of the old system and failure to rival the developments in the west. The aims are also clear: the transition to the western world's economic organisation, verified and based on market mechanisms, together with its widely understood system of values. It is however, extremely difficult to foresee details or elements of this process. The collapse of the organisational structures previously uniting the east European countries in May 1991 - i.e. the winding up of the CMEA - resulted in each of these countries following their own largely independent path. A specific degree of interdependence continues to exist between them in various economic sectors. The ties between them were formed over decades, and were frequently encouraged by such natural conditions as geographical situation, the distribution of mineral deposits, tradition and experience, and specialisation in specific fields of production. Each of these countries however, is now becoming increasingly more independent, a trend supported by increased political freedom and a desire to be seen to be moving away from the old, established regime. For these amongst other reasons, differences in the countries formerly belonging to the Eastern bloc, will increase rather than decrease. There does however, remain, and will continue to do so, a wide range of similarities that in many cases these countries will continue to exhibit and which justify the subject and scope of this paper.

The paper is divided into three parts: the past, present and future, and it is in these three planes that we shall try to acquaint the reader with some of the problems of shipping in this part of Europe. It is easiest to present the past, the present slightly more difficult, but the future presents sizeable problems. However, there are two reasons for attempting to do so; firstly because the processes taking place in these countries are not simultaneous in terms of their progress, which means that the specific character of each country has to be kept in mind so that the experience of one may be repeated or at least utilised by another; secondly, the more obscure the future, the greater the need to foresee it.

The past

None of the east European countries can be numbered among the group of so-called traditional maritime states. In the nineteenth and early twentieth centuries a modern world freight market emerged and an international division of labour was formed in shipping. This changed little over the following decades and, for various reasons, none of the east European states participated in these processes. In any case, most of these countries could not be found on the nineteenth century map of Europe.

The reasons for the absence of Russia from the traditional shipping nations at this time were different. Despite the numerous outstanding achievements in terms of Russian maritime discoveries, particularly fruitful in the sea routes of the Arctic and the Far North, the development of the merchant marine was poor, especially considering the potential of the Tsar's empire.

Some slight progress in the development of merchant fleets in eastern Europe was noted in the inter-war period. With substantial participation of state capital, Poland began to build up her merchant fleet based on the newly opened port at Gdynia. The beginnings of a fleet emerged in Yugoslavia, Romania and Bulgaria. Lacking direct access to the sea, Czechoslovakia and Hungary did not bother to expand their fleets. Lithuania, Latvia and Estonia did show some interest in this field; however, the overall activities of these states was hardly noticeable on the international shipping arena and the seaborne trade of the east European states was mainly carried out by traditional maritime countries - the United Kingdom, Germany and Scandinavia.

The years immediately following World War II revealed little progress in the development of the merchant fleets of the Eastern bloc states. The cold war did not favour the development of East West trade relations. The autarkic tendencies of the USSR during the inter-war period gradually embraced all countries falling within the orbit of Soviet influence and which eventually became members of the CMEA. Although increasing rapidly, mutual trade exchange within the bloc was mainly served by other transport means - in view of the geographical situation and flows of goods - so that seaborne transport accounted for only a small part of the carriage. This did not favour the development of merchant fleets in these countries, neither did the accepted economic policies, irrespective of their specific conditions and needs, nor the general shortage of capital together with steadily growing requirements for competing economic sectors.

All this means that the first half of the century, almost until the end of the 1950s, was unfavourable for the development of the merchant fleets in the USSR and other east European countries. Substantial progress in this field was noted in the 1960s and 1970s, and in certain countries also during the 1980s. During these decades a very rapid development took place of tonnage in CMEA country fleets. This resulted in the fleets playing an increasing role in the international freight market. The rate of their development considerably outpaced both that of the world fleet as a whole and that of traditional maritime nations. Further, the rate of development was faster as compared with that of the trade exchange of those countries and thus the rate of increase of carriage demands. This meant primarily an increase in the extent to which carriage requirements by own fleets were covered, and secondly - an increased supply of carriage services on various other markets by their owners and increased export carriage services on their part i.e. increased crosstrade carriage.

Growing competition from east European flags on certain trade routes was sometimes considered dangerous for the functioning of freight market mechanisms by west European shipping operators and policy-makers. The subject of suspicion was the state form of ownership in these fleets and the consequential related form of shipping protectionism.

What were the motives behind the development of merchant fleets in these countries and what aims were they to serve? To look for an answer to such questions in autarkical tendencies does not fully answer the question and would undoubtedly, substantially simplify the issue, although the frequently expressed need to 'be independent of foreign owners' might suggest close association with an autarkical policy.

A more detailed analysis of the problem facilitates analysis of the motives behind and the objectives of developing national merchant fleets in eastern Europe. These motives and objectives can be divided into two groups. One would include those common for all countries in the group and thus with a similar or identical argument embracing the need and purpose to develop their own merchant fleets. In this case emphasis is placed upon the economic beneficial effects afforded to the economy of the country by its merchant fleet. The role of the fleet in protection and promotion of the country's balance of payments is usually advanced: a domestic fleet averts currency expenditure in favour of foreign owners and may constitute a source of currency earnings for carriage on behalf of foreign owners. Given poor exports and continuous import demands, the inconvertibility of the CMEA countries' currencies gave rise to a constant demand to protect the balance of payments, hence the role of the fleet in this respect formed a powerful argument for fleet promotion. For similar motives, one can mention the aim to increase participation of the domestic fleet in serving the carriage demands of foreign trade, the possibility of exerting influence on the level of freight rates etc.. The importance of the fleet in building up national income, diversification of the economy, creating qualified specialist jobs - such arguments had no features, specific particularly to a centralised planned economy. They could equally well occur in any country, irrespective of its political system.

The second group of conditions and objectives of the development of merchant fleets in east European countries should include considerations specific to the given country. It is difficult to state whether their significance was supplementary or - in some cases - decisive. In either case, these particular conditions cannot be omitted. Let us try to point out some of them, and let us commence with the largest tonnage group - the merchant fleet of the USSR.

It would be difficult not to consider the relationships between the development of the USSR merchant fleet and that country's policies on a global scale i.e. the policies of an international power which began to play the role of one of the main factors of the post-war political and military equilibrium in the world. The USSR's interests and influence gradually moved beyond the area lying within its terrestrial range and reached out to overseas lands.

One could note that the USSR's overseas expansion in the second half of the twentieth century differed essentially from that of the developed European countries in the eighteenth and nineteenth centuries. At that time, the basis of the expansionist activities of England, France, Germany or the USA a little later - backed up by powerful navies and merchant fleets - were *par excellence* economic considerations. Secondary motives were political, ideological and religious considerations. In the case of the USSR expansion, goals of an ideological and political nature were to the fore, economic considerations being secondary they were to facilitate the former. As it later proved, the majority of costs were borne in the economic sphere and there were only transitory gains in the spheres of politics and ideology.

As a result of the USSR being engaged at various times in North Korea, Vietnam, Cuba, Nicaragua, Angola, Ethiopia, Afghanistan and attempts to gain influence in the Arab world, the country's politics assumed global features. This weakened rather than strengthened the Soviet Union. From the present position, it can be clearly concluded that the export of ideology was a highly unremunerative activity. It intensified what was only already an ineffective system of centralised economic management.

In any case, the pursuance of a global policy politically and ideologically, necessitated the availability of a merchant fleet of suitable size and structure, and hence its development. Russia, and later the USSR, traditionally a continental power, became also a marine power in the second half of the twentieth century. An attribute of this power was not just the navy but also the merchant fleet.

Analogies between the extra economic motivation for the development of appropriately large and efficient merchant fleets by the two great powers - the USA and USSR - are too obvious not to be noted here. Whereas, however, in the case of the USA this was and is part of the official maritime and strategic doctrine (the merchant fleet is treated as a 'forth arm') in the case of the USSR the economic premises of the development of the merchant fleet were always emphasised and all other reasons for its development rather avoided, not to say camouflaged, in official publications (e.g. Gorszkow, S. 1979 *The Maritime Power of a Modern State*. Polish Edition, Warsaw p55).

Without doubt, these types of particular circumstances which can be attributed to the Soviet Union, did not exist in eastern Europe but other specific motives for development can be observed. In Poland, for example, the population was particularly sensitive - in a positive sense - to the development of a maritime economy, particularly the merchant fleet. The social climate favoured this. It originated, to a certain extent, from Poland's historical experiences, of how the question of access to the sea took shape in the past and the powerful connections between access to the sea and the country's independence. Thus matters related to the sea stood high in the Poles' hierarchy of values. This was strengthened by the changes in Poland's borders after World War II and gaining a much longer sea coast with several large ports. This new situation which favoured the development of a merchant fleet became the ambition, not only of the authorities, but also the people. It is worth adding that higher education and specialist maritime training had also greatly developed - perhaps more than expected of a country of Poland's size and trading connections. This encouraged the formation of a strong lobby, which undoubtedly played a specific role in investment decisions and the rapid development of the merchant fleet in the 1960s and 1970s. Conducive to this was the substantial development of Poland's shipbuilding industry.

In the former GDR, the function of the merchant fleet was specifically transport of foreign trade, defence, balance of payments contribution, a source of national income and the security function consisting of fulfilling the tasks of the country's foreign policy (Breitzman, 1991). The first three functions constituted the economic conditions for fleet development and as noted earlier, these motivations for fleet development existed in all CMEA countries. The fourth function was particularly important when the GDR was a young state and exhibiting attributes of independence, when sovereignty was important for international contacts, especially in expanding contacts with Third World countries. A national merchant fleet was one such attribute.

In the case of Bulgaria and Romania, the motives for the development of merchant fleets were similar to those of other countries. An additional impulse in Bulgaria might have been the development of the shipbuilding industry as from the 1970s. In Romania, the aim of achieving as high a degree of transport independence as possible in the carriage of imports and exports, may have played a greater role than in the other countries of this group. This can be ascribed to Romanian economic policy in the 1970s, when her ties with CMEA countries, particularly the Soviet Union, slackened in favour of closer contacts with the West and developing countries. Romania became the only European member of the group of developing countries in the United Nations with the benefits in trading terms this brings.

Two countries not having access to the sea - Czechoslovakia and Hungary - also had their own merchant fleets. They were only small and despite spatial drawbacks, their development may have been justified by both economic considerations and the tendency towards at least symbolic independence in as many economic fields as possible, including the seaborne merchant fleet.

The development by all CMEA countries of their own merchant fleets might have given the impression that the organisation had not followed the principles of international division of labour and specialisation in production too strictly among its members. The process and structure of maritime transport adopted in each of these states was never exactly the same although there remained many similarities and correlations. Differences arose from many internal and external sources, economic, as well as social and political.

Today

It is impossible to analyse in detail, or even in general terms, the present state of the merchant fleets of each east European country, as this would exceed the volume and scope of this paper. We shall therefore discuss only certain problems which the fleets face as a result of the changes taking place in East Europe. Similar problems occur in each country, as they have derived from similar economic and social systems whilst certain differences between the countries also exist, of course, in such characteristics as area, population, history and tradition, as well as in economic, social, political and cultural aspects.

As regards shipping matters, the differences in problems manifest themselves in scale, importance, degree of advancement of solution, type of difficulty and the existence of barriers. Any generalisation assumed in this part of the discussion is justified by the numerous common features between particular countries and the general situation overall of their merchant fleets. At the same time, it is realised that generalisations so formulated may not reflect the true situation to the same degree at each time in each country, partly at least because of the rate of change taking place which is not identical in each state.

The basic problem is the diminishing demand for seaborne carriage in foreign trade. The reason for this is the decrease in production in almost all fields of industry and also in agriculture in some countries. The extent of this has fluctuated notably in recent years and in the case of Poland and the Czech Republic, may now be reversed. The sources of these decreases very: the cessation of subsidies for unprofitable branches of production by the state, internal and external decrease in demand, the opening up of the economy, outside capital and import competition, weakening or decline of production cooperation within the former CMEA, lack of capital for modernisation of industry and hence the use of out-of-date technology, fulfilment of anti-inflation programmes etc. Whilst each of these reasons has its own source the cumulative effect also is important as the influence of one cause gives rise to or consolidates the others. The direct effect of a fall in production or the diminishing turnover of foreign goods manifesting itself as falls in imports and exports, results inevitably in a drop in cargo turnover in ports and demand for seaborne carriage services. Trade exchange between the Soviet Union and east European countries constituted a substantial share of their total trade turnovers. A drop in trade activities in each, thus reflects severely on turnovers which were previously high. As the share of the domestic merchant fleet in serving national ports was high, hence the collapse of turnovers automatically resulted in a fall in demand for the services of domestic owners. For them, this meant a drop in carriage and thus income from freight. Another effect may be reduction of tonnage (the sale of ships, laying up etc.), unless owners are able to obtain cargoes on the international freight market, thus compensating through an additional supply.

Poland is an excellent example of the scale of change. In the past, carriage by Poland's fleet was made up of one third crosstrade, two thirds domestic trade. These proportions have been reversed, crosstrade constituting about two thirds of total carriage. The changes in proportions in other countries are not necessarily so drastic, but the direction of change is the same.

These changes will alter the ratio between the share of the USSR and east European countries in world trade exchange and share of the world merchant fleets. In 1988, this group's share in world turnovers (goods loaded) was 5.8% and share of tonnage of the world merchant fleet (DWT) 6.9% (Review of Maritime Transport, 1989). Consequently, world shipping did not fear substantial competition from these fleets, nor disruption of the balance between supply and demand in the freight market. The situation may be easier or more difficult depending upon the tonnage groups and routes and thus the influence on the market may be greater or less. It should be stressed that part of the available tonnage has competed on the crosstrade market for years.

Another problem consists of deterioration of the average technical standard of these fleets, leading to an unsatisfactory degree of modernisation. Stagnation in the development of tonnage recently has been due to the slow down of tonnage renewal processes and the failure to replace old tonnage with new, profitable and effective units. In some cases, the withdrawal of old units has not been accompanied by the purchase of new ones resulting, of course, in a diminution of tonnage size.

The percentage of old ships in the fleets is high. In 1988, 29.3% of the ships in the CMEA transport fleet were over 16 years. In the Bulgarian fleet this figure was 23.9%, in the Czechoslovakian 47.6%, the GDR 32.9%, Polish 26.5%, Hungarian 41.2%, and the USSR 34.0%. Only 23% of the tonnage of these states consisted of ships under 5 years (Acc. Morsky, 1989). These indices have deteriorated in recent years which hinders profitable employment on the international market and makes the fleet less competitive. The reason for this unfavourable state of affairs is a shortage of the necessary financial means for the purchase of new tonnage.

In the centralised economic system, profits from state owned enterprises, including shipping, were accumulated by a central state authority, which later distributed them in accordance with, among other things, the central investment plan. Growing difficulties in the whole economy meant that shipping enterprises did not receive the money they had earned. The result was that these enterprises commonly had insufficient funds and the central power did not award additional funds for investment. Irrespective of the reasons for this state of affairs, the tonnage modernisation process was substantially slowed down or even abandoned due to the shortage of necessary capital.

Even the elimination of central control of the economy, which has already taken place in the majority of countries of this group and which will continue where it is still in the initial phase, is unable to improve the owners' situation quickly. Not always, and not everywhere are they capable of the independent accumulation of capital reserves for new investment, the moreso as their financial troubles do not end there. Constantly increasing economic difficulties in these countries rule out the chances of finding adequate capital resources needed to renew tonnage, the economy or its banking system - especially relevant to credits and credit guarantees.

Irrespective of the problems connected with the shortage of financial means for investment, another of today's problems may be the owner's current financial difficulties. The economic reforms carried out in these countries have now reached the point where commonly, the situation is unfavourable for state owned enterprises. Difficulties arise in the payment of freight by domestic shippers - often still state owned firms - as the result of financial difficulties stemming from reformation of the economy. Inflation readjustments are painful for shipowners, and strengthening the domestic currency by its partial convertibility to fight inflation pressures (for example in Poland) results in the rapid increase of domestic costs, given freight returns in convertible currencies. The depreciation by some countries of rates of exchange which were previously oversestimated in relation to convertible currencies, means that the accounts of enterprises operating on the international market are more acceptable. In certain situations, centrally controlled fluctuations in currency exchange rates may be unfavourable for domestic shipowners.

The problem which , in some countries, may be of essential importance for the shipowners' financial situation, is the changing financial status of state owned enterprises. There is, unfortunately, a shortage of more detailed information on the basis of which the financial independence, or lack of this, in the shipowning enterprises of particular countries, could be analysed. It is thus impossible to assess whether government policies in relation to shipping now embrace such steps as the adoption of direct or indirect subsidies, compensation or other forms of financial assistance. These matters were frequently the subject of disputes between western shipping interests and east European shipowners. Accusations addressed to the latter were commonly concerned with various forms of protectionism which resulted from ignorance of the totally different financial principles in force in state enterprises within a centralised system of management, artificial currency conversion rates, complex and not often unstable taxation systems, etc.

The present situation in Poland, for example, is that state owned shipping enterprises are fully independent, operating on commercial principles in relation to both foreign and domestic shippers. The centrally established parameter is the current rate of exchange of domestic in relation to convertible foreign currency and internal convertibility of domestic currency. Shipowning enterprises are taxed similarly to other state owned enterprises. These taxes are considerably higher those on average in western Europe and there are no reductions for shipping enterprises. Further, no forms of subsidy are available in accordance with the general trends of reforms in the economy. Under the reforms, subsidies for unprofitable enterprises were eliminated and, as regards the tax system, all fields of the economy were treated similarly. No cargo preferences are applied in Poland, thus, generally speaking, a fully liberalised market exists in shipping, such as is rarely noted in this form in highly developed traditional maritime countries.

Even if the state shipping enterprise situation in other east European countries is not identical, the direction of reforms is very similar and it can be assumed that the functioning of shipowning enterprises should be based upon market principles. With the opening up of the economy of these countries to the outside world, the introduction of new currency exchange rates, freedom of economic activity, and development of private entrepreneurship or privatisation of state owned enterprises, this will lead to a substantial participation of Poland's domestic fleet in covering the demands of foreign trade. The earlier arguments to protect the balance of payments and other priorities from the state point of view are gradually declining in importance. The purely commercial criterion, that of an enterprise with its objectives set primarily upon profit, is coming to the fore to an ever increasing degree.

The shipowners, who treat their partners - state owned enterprises - on fully commercial principles, represent the same trend of thinking. They may refuse their carriage services if the customer is in financial difficulty, or if more profitable employment for ships is available on the market (Komieranst, 1991). This commercialisation of relations between domestic owners and shippers is not entirely new in certain countries (e.g. Poland) as it was adopted to a considerable extent in the last years of the communist regime.

We have touched upon the next problem which is growing in importance, that is the privatising of state owned enterprises, which occupies a leading position in the reform of the state economy. The rate at which this is carried out is an index of the progress and success of the reforms. The degree of advancement of the process depends upon numerous and various factors and the rate of changes of ownership in this group of countries differs. Poland, Hungary and the Czech Republic are the most advanced; possibly Romania, the Central Asian Republics and Ukraine the least. The scale of the problem is tremendous. As regards the position of shipowning enterprises there are, as yet, no final or fixed decisions or solutions adopted. The merchant fleet will certainly not be the sector of the economy which will lead the privatisation of enterprises. There are several reasons for this, the most important being: high capital requirements of shipping enterprises, relative uncompetitiveness on the international market, and slender possibilities of development of the "employee-shareholder" concept. The latter stems from the very high value of tonnage compared with the number of employees.

Another reason for the slow rate of privatisation in shipping may be the shortage of domestic capital and interest on the part of foreign capital in investing in the shipping enterprises of these countries, particularly if other fields of the economy afford more advantageous conditions. If we also consider the lack of tradition of private shipping enterprises, which resulted from the development of the merchant fleet in Poland during the inter-war period utilising only state capital, then we are faced with several essential constraints which do not favour early privatisation in shipping.

Preparatory work is, however, under way and this can be treated as the first phase in the privatisation processes. This is the transformation of state owned shipping enterprises into commercial law companies in which initially, the treasury is the owner of the shares, but the ownership structure - i.e. the shareholders - may change without any formal legal action based on the purchase and sale of shares.

A separate problem worthy of note, is the relationship of east European owners to open registers. In the past, registration of ships in such registers was rare, but interest in this option is increasing. Russian and Polish owners provide examples of this. The motives of changing registers is a question of gaining operational conditions for ships which enable cost cutting, particularly of the tax burden. Not without importance is the reduction of crew numbers, which is difficult under the domestic flag due to trade union resistance.

There may be other resistance to flags of convenience, as an outflow of tonnage means a diminishing influx of taxes to the state treasury. With the fairly common difficulties in balancing budgets or budget deficits in east European countries, additional sources of income are sought and existing ones are not rejected without considerable thought. The degree of a firm's independence and consequential lack of alternatives, influences decisions about whether shipowning enterprises are to stay in the market.

A drop in operational tonnage gives rise to another problem, partly connected with flags of convenience, namely, as the number of east European seafarers employed on foreign ships - mainly flags of convenience - increases. Allowing free choice by employers of seafarers from any nationality may result, in some cases, in a rapid rise in crew costs for east European owners, if they wish to avoid difficulties in manning their ships. Such a situation has arisen already in Poland, for example.

To conclude the general comments on current problems of east European shipping, it is worth noting another issue. This is, the variety of organisational forms in which shipping enterprises exist and function. The operations of the CMEA did not lead to unification in this respect and this was never intended. The differences emerged even though the companies operated under the same system of management in a centralised economy based upon state ownership and the functions of enterprises within it. The differences have their source in certain traditions including the desire and tendencies to transfer and apply models existing in the USSR and the tradition of those systems existing in the past etc.. We thus have to deal with different solutions including a greater or lesser degree of concentration of tonnage in one enterprise and specialisation of enterprises in one type of shipping or their diversification. In certain cases, the management of seaports or ship repair yards was also in the hands of shipping enterprises. In others there were intermediary structures with various functions and ranges of operation. The central body of decision at government level was and is differently constituted with independent ministries of shipping, sometimes falling under the Ministry of Transport or of Foreign Trade or, even in one case, the Treasury.

Irrespective of these differences, there existed and, to a considerable degree still exists, a certain commonality of shipping enterprises in these countries. Apart from functions related to the commercial operation of ships, in which they basically differ from other shipping enterprises in the world, they were burdened with several additional functions, which never existed on such a scale in western shipowners' enterprises. These included (and in a few cases still do include), the extensive and varied social and training functions and facilities, personnel departments, staff reserves, supply departments, with related and inland internal transport sections, research centres, publishing departments etc. This resulted in a widely extended management system, an increased number of employees in the administration, and thus pushed up costs, with a negative effect on overall financial results and in addition, diluted the activities of what were primarily ship operating companies into activities outside their specific expertise.

The changes at present taking place in the organisation of shipping enterprises constitute the beginning of the process which is to lead to the rationalisation of employment and will relieve organisational structures from all kinds of auxiliary and non-productive functions. Certain functions can be, and have already been in some cases, placed in the hands of specific enterprises employed on their own account to operate these ancillary activities.

The extent to which changes are advanced in shipowning organisations and structures varies in different countries and depends upon the rate of the overall process of reforming the whole economy. Without changes in this field, it would be difficult to imagine the solution of certain other problems, such as, privatisation, joint ventures involving the influx of foreign capital, or keeping pace with market competition in gaining cargoes from foreign shippers.

The future

It is extremely difficult to give even a general outline of the future facing the east European merchant fleets. One could try to grasp certain possible, though not inevitable trends, but any attempt to place these and their effects in time is almost hopeless. This is the case because of the acceptance of a simple and what would seem almost unquestionable rule, that in each of these countries, the situation of the merchant fleet depends on the overall economic situation. It is here that the circle closes as predictions as to the general state of the economy in this part of Europe are even more difficult. The reason for the difficulties in forecasting are simple: the transition from a socialist economy based on state ownership and a centralised system of command and distribution, to a capitalist economy based upon private ownership and market mechanisms, is not based on a set of well defined theoretical bases or practical experience. It is essentially experimental. The effects of steps taken may differ from those expected, assumptions may not be confirmed in practice and not all correlations of economic phenomena and processes can be foreseen and accepted as assumed to be correct.

In these countries, the development of long term plans has receded into the background under the pressure of present day problems. What is more, most of these plans - even short term - drawn up so far have proved unacceptable or incorrect after a matter of months. More significant plans drawn up by such centres as the International Monetary Fund or the World Bank have proved wildly inaccurate in respect of short term forecasts with the differences between true and forecast values sometimes considerable. As regards long term forecasts, the range of opinions and assessments is so great that they are unreliable from the beginning. It is easier to understand this state of affairs if we realise that the overall programme of reforms needed to achieve the target of a market economy is not obvious. The target is not questioned by the great majority of theoreticians, practitioners and enterprises in east European countries. There are, on the other hand, different opinions in each of the countries as to the rate at which reforms should progress, for instance, and whether a "shock" or "evolutionary" method is better. Can success be attained by minimising the negative social effects, will the population sustain the cost of reforms, and which social groups should bear the greatest burden of costs? Various answers to these and many similar questions have been formulated by specialists, experts and representatives of various political forces commonly with the underlying motive of winning votes.

Even in the case of the unification of Germany it turned out that the initial assessment of the rate and degree of unification needed of the former GDR with the rest of Germany proved unrealisable and the whole process of reforms, although overall in a more advantageous situation than the other east European countries, under the wing of the wealthy and highly developed state of the Federal Republic, will have to be spread over a much longer period than initially assumed.

It is not always possible to benefit from the experience of other countries in view of the specific conditions which may be found in each. The reforms in the huge, and at present both complicated and disrupted economic mechanism of the FSU will differ from each of the other states. The state of advancement of the reforms in particular countries differs; it is highest in Poland, Hungary and ex-Czechoslovakia, less advanced are Bulgaria and Romania, with ex-Yugoslavia and the FSU affording a different set of problems. Economic change in each state may be attained by passing through similar stages but differently distributed over time.

It can be assumed that the process of further shaping the economic situation in this part of Europe will develop in three consecutive phases. The first - worsening recession, second stagnation, third acceleration of development.

Poland is currently undergoing the second phase moving into the third, there having been a drop in production, foreign trade exchange and increased unemployment. Radical reforms commenced in the last phase. There has been a drop in the role of the central state, greater independence given to enterprises, commencement of ownership changes (privatisation), reform of the banking system, anti inflation measures, and an opening up of the economy to the outside, which may be accompanied by initial changes in the direction of trade exchange. The initial depressed stage was followed by a brief period of stagnation and now appears to be moving rapidly towards the first signs of economic growth The trade turnover between the ex-CMEA countries has dropped, particularly trade exchange between the FSU and other countries in the region and in the first and second phases there occurred a growing necessity to replenish capital from outside and a certain influx of capital from bilateral agreements or from international financial institutions. Depending upon the rate of changes accepted, the first phase may last from three to five years, or even longer. Only really in Poland and the Czech Republic has this first phase been concluded although there are signs that this may now be the case in Hungary as well. Other states - e.g. Slovakia, Romania and Bulgaria began the process of reform slightly later, whilst the other countries of the region (e.g. Moldova, Ukraine, the Baltic States etc.), have experienced an even slower rate of change so far.

The situation of the merchant fleets may further deteriorate in this initial phase of reform, as the unfavourable trends mentioned in 'Today' will continue. Thus the domestic cargo base may continue to fall, as may the fleet tonnage due to the ageing of ships and their withdrawal from operation. Lack of capital for modernisation of tonnage may force owners to abandon certain activities and concentrate diminishing financial facilities to maintain and possibly modernise those tonnage groups which realise the best results. In particular situations, this may mean departing from serving domestic shippers in favour of crosstrade work.

In the first phase, shipowning enterprises have in general, taken steps to rationalise organisational structures, reduce employment of men on board ships and ashore and disencumber firms from additional functions. The international freight market also had an increasing influence on the owners' situation. The greater the share of crosstrade in total carriage, the greater the owners' sensitivity to market fluctuations. During this period the government approach to shipping varied. The general direction consisted of the gradual (or sudden) disappearance of all forms of aid and preferences, if such existed, and in increasing liberalisation of shipping policy.

In the second phase - i.e. stagnation - slow down of the recession should be expected followed by a halt in the fall in production and foreign trade turnovers. There may be a slight increase of 1-2% annually. The process of basic reforms should conclude. There should be a decisive change in ownership with private ownership prevailing. The process of banking reform should have been concluded and the strengthening of domestic currency well advanced (with a minimum achievement of full convertibility domestically). In certain countries (Poland, Hungary, the Czech Republic) the process of rapprochement with the EU countries may be advanced by appropriate changes in legislation, trade policy, customs policy - which will result from the status of the associated countries. In this phase of changes restructuring of production should take place e.g. winding up of enterprises and even commercial sectors which do not manufacture competitive goods on the market and where the modernisation and development of those enterprises would have little impact upon their prospects of competition in the international marketplace.

As the result of the restructuring process which is occurring with varying intensity in different countries, a degree of stabilisation should occur in the extent, structure and direction of trade exchange with abroad and it is possible that exchange between these countries and with the FSU will once again appear to a limited extent. On the other hand, there may be a drop in turnover with developing countries. The reasons may include difficulties in crediting exports, the diminishing of non economic motives for trade exchange due to the necessity to restructure the economy (particularly in the FSU), the introduction of modernisation processes, the need to catch up with advances in techniques and technology taking place worldwide etc.. During this phase, conditions will most certainly arise increasing trade exchange with western Europe, the USA and countries of south east Asia and examples of this are already clearly occurring.

The phase of stagnation, embracing the economic reconstruction processes required for further development, may last from four to seven years. As in the case of the first phase, the time taken may vary in different countries, which will depend on the level achieved in present day economic development, the degree of recession in the first place, as well as the acceptable and attained rate of reform. The influx of foreign capital will have a substantial influence on the rate and success of changes taking place in the second phase. In this phase, the capital demands will be considerably greater than in phase one and to a substantial degree connected with the restriction of production potential, but the liabilities of these countries to their creditors in the West will not diminish during this period.

What effect will the latter phase of development have on the merchant fleets ?

Primarily, their position in the reformed economic structure should be clarified. If it proves that owners can maintain their position based on the international market, then the chances of operating and developing under the national flag will increase, particularly with the growth of seaborne trade. These fleets may be faced on the one side with changes in the structure of demand for carriage services, and on the other, greater competition from foreign flags, in serving domestic shippers' cargoes. In the first case this may result from changes in the production structure and hence that of imports and exports. In the second case, the reason may be liberalisation of relations between shippers and owners, creating purely economic relationships between them, as well as greater attraction of demand for carriage services in the ports of these countries.

The latter will be opportune particularly when with the reshaping and restructuring of the whole economy, the efficiency of handling of ships in the ports improves and the cargoes available stabilise. It is quite conceivable that by then some tonnage will have been registered with one of the open registers and thus its connection with domestic ports will be more flexible.

In this phase of development the privatisation of enterprises and their possible connections with foreign capital should be clarified. It is difficult to state whether the participation of private capital will be substantial but most probably not, unless this is foreign capital. It may be that as regards the form of ownership, joint stock companies will predominate, with a greater or lesser share of state capital, which is probable in the case of large fleets. It will probably be easier to privatise smaller groups of tonnage. During this period, shipowning enterprises should conclude the process of changing their structures and range of activities and will thus not differ in this respect from western European owners. The general policies of these east European states as regards shipping, should be similar to the principles adopted in EU countries.

The phases of development of the economy and shipping enterprises which have been outlined above, may together last from seven to twelve years. It should be stressed that successful reformation of the economy in the next ten years will depend upon several factors. These include: a stable political situation for each country, the full support of society, and an influx of foreign capital. The latter requires overcoming three barriers: first - gaining sources of capital, second - preparing the economy for the rational absorption of such capital, third - solving the problem of liabilities, which will increase in the first and second phases rather than decrease. It would be best if the influx of capital were not in the form of loans or aid which does not need to be repaid but in the form of investment, capital joint ventures with domestic enterprises etc. A lot will, of course, depend on the situation of the world economy.

In the phase of economic revitalisation, the rate of economic development should be higher that the rate of development of west European countries if the differences between the two parts of Europe are to lessen. For east European countries to attain today's average level of those of the EU will take, given favourable conditions, at least one generation. We are generalising substantially here. East and west European countries differ as regards level of economic development, consumption patterns, productivity, etc.. We do not assume that all the east European states, including the FSU, will carry out their reforms and develop at the same rate. We are also of the opinion that the possibility of some East European countries becoming full members of the EU will depend on the success reached in the third phase of development. This will almost certainly happen in the twenty-first century.

What will be the prospects for shipping in eastern Europe in the third phase of development ? This is easier to answer, despite the fact that it concerns a distant and hence uncertain future. As compared with the first and second phases, the prospects are most favourable. This is true, of course, for the fleets which have overcome the difficulties of the first and second phase scenarios. An economic boom will mean a growth in trade exchange and demand for services. The fleet will base its activities on healthy and sustainable factors. Economic considerations plus tradition, experience and knowledge of the market will place domestic owners in a competitive position with respect to domestic shippers. East European ports will also have a richer and more attractive offer to present to foreign owners, whose share in carriage will probably be much higher than at present. Where the market situation is good, conditions for the development and modernisation of tonnage to catch up with the world average, will be that much better. In what condition will the east European shipowners survive ? Time will show. We can expect to see certain losses during the reformation period and the degree to which the difficulties of the next few years will be overcome will vary. In the best situation will be those who based their operations on economic principles in the past and continue to do so in the future and whose cargo acquisition is based on the international freight market. In a worse situation will be those who benefit from various forms of state assistance, either in the form of financial advantages or facilitating access to domestic cargoes.

In trying to gain an insight into the future of shipping in east Europe, we unavoidably come up with the questions "will it be possible to maintain and develop merchant fleets which can successfully compete with the fleets of other states on the international freight market based on purely economic principles, without the assistance and protection of the state ? Would it be possible for these states to develop fleets directed mainly towards the crosstrades, as in Norway or Greece ?"

Certain circumstances suggest a positive answer to these questions. These include: their extensive existing tonnage and many years experience in its operation: own, highly qualified crews and operators; domestic, well developed shipbuilding industries in some of the countries - for example Romania, Bulgaria and Poland; a well developed ship-repair industry; domestic, experienced shipbroking and forwarding agents; own nautical and shipping education facilities with a well developed maritime transport and shipbuilding research technical back-

68

up; long standing connections between liner owners, liner conference systems and shippers from numerous countries; and lower costs of manpower as compared with the highly developed countries. These and similar circumstances suggest favourable conditions. Any barriers and liabilities are rooted in the faults of the economic system to which shipping has been tied for many years. It was simultaneously a part of this system and the market system burdened with the faults of an ineffective command-distribution system and centralised state economy. It simultaneously accumulated experience and developed the ability to work in the conditions of the international market. The relinquishing of these negative burdens is thus easier in shipping than in other fields of the economy that have not had such direct connections with the international market. This creates a certain priority for shipping in the restructuring processes which will take place in the economies of these countries.

As previously mentioned, the east European countries do not have the centuries-old traditions that some of those constituting the leaders in shipping in the contemporary world enjoy. History shows that tradition - although commonly having a positive influence - plays an ever decreasing role in the international division of labour. This is confirmed, for example, in the shift, during the last dozen or so years, of the main centres of shipbuilding or the success of the development of new fields of production to the newly industrialised countries of south east Asia, with no traditions in this field. It is sometimes the case that the longer the tradition, the stronger the enterprise is tied to the past, so hindering suitable future progress for the industry.

In conclusion, the discussions in this paper justify a certain amount of optimism, although in the more distant, rather than near future. Only time will tell which east European shipping industry or industries will survive and prosper and which will fade and die.

References

Breitzman K.H. (1991) Transition from a planned to market economy: problems, tasks, and first results in shipping of East Germany. In *Current issues in Maritime Economics*. International Conference at the Erasmus University, Rotterdam, the Netherlands.

Review of Maritime Transport (1989) Report of the UNCTAD Sectretariat, Geneva TD/B/C4/344, pp5 and 12.

Acc. Morsky transporting flot stran - chlenov SEW (1989), Moscow, Russia.

Komieranst (1991), Moscow, August edition.

The impact of Poland's political and economic changes upon the shipping sector

Michal Rosa
Former vice-Director Polish Ocean Lines

Abstract

This paper takes a practical look at the position of Polish Ocean Lines - the principle state liner operator - just prior to the major structural changes that have occurred in the company since 1990/1991.

Introduction

In recent years, significant political and economic changes have taken place in Poland. The results of elections to the National Assembly have demonstrated the popularity of new ideas and programmes. Society, however, expects much from government solutions, which, apart from releasing the human initiative, facilitating and accelerating economic activity, would also intensify foreign trade and subsequently, shipping. This paper looks at the position of the major state owned liner operator - Polish Ocean Lines (POL) - just prior to these major changes in 1990/1991.

Polish Ocean Lines

POL is a well known name in the international shipping world. Founded in 1950, as a state ocean carrier located in Gdynia, the company has established a strong presence in the liner market, with a global network covering virtually all major regions, with over 100 vessels at its disposal.

As early as 1969, POL started to carry containers on the UK route and in 1972, established a container department, later afforded a divisional status.

The company's container activities built up steadily, relying initially on a mix of break bulk and semi container tonnage, then receiving purpose built specialised units. Since the early 1980s, POL had accelerated substantially its path into the container era, adapting fleet and management structures to the new market challenge. This re-organisation facilitated the task of coordinating the operation of 21 lines, each with substantial freedom of action, thus allowing for a more efficient employment of POL resources.

POL liner connections were grouped as follows:

America and Australia services:

      - North Atlantic Con/Ro Service
      - South America West Coast Line
      - South America East Coast Line
      - Australia Line Ro/Ro Service

Asia, South Pacific, Mediterranean and Red Sea Services:

      - Far East Line
      - South Pacific Line
      - Indonesia-Vietnam Line
      - India, Pakistan, Arab Gulf Line

- Bengal Line
- Red Sea Line
- Mediterranean Service

Europe and West Africa Services:

- Great Britain and Ireland Lines
- West European Lines
- Rail/car Ferry Line Swinoujscie-Ystad
- West Africa Line

This was a truly world-wide network, providing shipments from Europe to practically all destinations at competitive prices. It involved some 2,150 shore based staff, with 5,500 at sea. Fifty owner representatives operated abroad and there were over 500 POL agents covering all ports of call.

In 1989, the fleet operated by POL totalled 100 units of some 1,000,000 DWT. The POL fleet could handle containers, ro/ro shipments, breakbulk, deeptank, reefer and all kinds of conventional cargo - altogether, some 5 million tonnes per year. Meanwhile the company's strategy for the end of the decade consisted of steady growth of the container capacity and continuous fleet modernisation.

The successive withdrawal of the old conventional units and delivery of the cellular and ro/ro newbuilding changed the fleet structure in favour of specialised ships, accounting in 1990, for 56% of POL tonnage (52 units). The company's fleet of owned and leased boxes at the end of 1989 was 34,393 TEU owned and 4,000 TEU leased units.

Their container capacity placed POL among the 20 largest container operators in the world at the beginning of the 1990s. Since the delivery of the first specialised ocean going vessels in 1989, the volume of containerised cargo carried by Polish Ocean Lines expanded rapidly. In 1988 POL carried 1,991.7 thousand tons of containerised cargo, accounting for 39.2% of the overall cargo volumes lifted by the company.

The planned delivery of 18 modern units during 1986-1990 enabled the radical reorganisation of several POL services. What was new in POL's offer ? Amongst the trades which increased their standards of performance, there were:

-2 regular lines with South America (East and West Coast), receiving since 1986, multipurpose tonnage of 'Warszawa II' type (13,635 DWT, 320 TEU);

-modernised connections from Szczecin and Gdynia to Finland, operating now ro/ro tonnage ('Puck' - 4,014 DWT, 225 TEU and 'Elblag' - 4,170

DWT, 180 TEU). Sailings of 'Elblag' were coordinated with the schedule of the hucke-pack train linking weekly Gdynia and Vienna;

-The traditional service to the Mediterranean received from 1987, five ro/ro units of 'Zeran' type (7,300 DWT, 490 TEU). These versatile ships offered a regular ten day service calling at Valetta, Limassol, Lattakia, Beirut, Mersin and Alexandria, while the needs of the western Mediterranean continued to be met by conventional lift-off/lift-on means;

-Swinoujscie-Ystad ferry line, strengthened in April 1988 through the delivery of the new rail/car ferry 'Jan Sniadecki' (5,100 DWT), with the option of the sister unit in the early 1990s;

-Far East Line, where POL and DSR Rostock started a container service ('EACON)' in July 1988.

Respective agreements provided for mutual slot exchange and employment of 13 full container ships within agreed and regular joint schedules. POL contributed three cellular, gearless units of B-355 class (22,800 DWT, 1,633 TEU). The prototype 'H.Cegielski' entered operation in August 1988. The 'EACON' service offered regular fortnightly sailings and its concept embodied extensive feeders with Gdynia, Rostock, Hamburg, Bremerhaven, Antwerp, Larnaca, Khor Fakkan, Colombo, Singapore and Hong Kong designated as transhipment centres for the respective geographical regions.

POL's growing commitment towards containerisation was irrevocably shifting its main objective from efficient fleet management in the traditional form, to a more sophisticated type of shipping and comprehensive inland organisation. With a ship renewal programme underway and a new management approach implemented, POL entered a period of consolidation, reflected in its financial standing. The company's determination to remain a leading operator meant a continuous effort to keep in step with changes occurring in international shipping business.

Obviously their hopes had to allow for Polish reality. Shipping continued to have, as in the past, a positive balance with respect to the state budget. This did not mean that shipping was not given any support from the government, but POL considered their government support to be small in comparison with some west European circumstances.

The biggest problem facing all Polish companies operating on the international market was the punitive official rate of exchange of the Polish currency to any free currency. For companies such as POL, which accounted for all their incomes and a substantial part of costs in free currency, even a small change in the rate of exchange had a considerable influence on financial results. POL hoped that normalisation in this field would quickly enter into force. Such a decision would have had, as well as a financial impact, also a great influence on international cooperation with shipowners. This point had been proven in the past, when a number of governmental and company initiatives amongst communist countries attempted to tighten cooperation between shipowners. All these projects collapsed due to lack of a common currency. Some of the agreements which survived had never been operational but had existed only in theory.

At a time when the Polish government was looking to reduce its involvement in companies' activities, the former were faced, for the first time, with the problem of survival. There were no real chances to privatise the larger companies due to the lack of capital on the domestic market.

Furthermore, the short term economy was unpredictable and was likely to be unstable. Many Polish economists predicted a decline of the national product. The big imbalance in the state budget and huge international debts forced the Polish government - both communist and non communist - to introduce a strict taxation policy toward both consumer and capital markets. Such ideology was possibly helped by the International Monetary Fund and World Bank programmes. In the author's opinion, the only way big companies did survive was to behave as many other west European firms used to do. As far as shipowners were concerned this involved moving to more convenient flags (tax wise) and to developing more efficient management systems. Both steps could have been, some experts say should have been, carried out in close cooperation with foreign partners.

The final changes in Polish shipping regulations provided the potential to change to alternative flags. POL also sought serious investors in the west, in order to form joint ventures. Their intention was to locate these new companies outside Poland. As a result of such a policy, the mother company in Poland could transform its activities from a traditional east European shipowner, to a modern west European style ship operator.

Practical tasks have already been described and some steps in this field were taken by 1991. For example only a part of POL's fleet was owned by POL as a number of their vessels had been transferred to their subsidiary, PTO. Some vessels were officially owned by a joint venture registered in Panama.

The other major practical movement which was under development was in computerisation. Parallel with the transformation of the organisational structure, POL installed a comprehensive computer network based upon Wang hardware. The software was developed by POL themselves. Greater use of computers was urgently needed, especially to assist container logistics. By 1991, POL was one of the most computerised companies in Poland and possibly in the ex-communist bloc.

Since January 1987, POL's internal organisation had undergone radical transformation. The previous structure resembled that of an association of semi-independent liner divisions, while by 1987 all liner services were subordinated to the Executive Director of Shipping.

Another very delicate problem concerned employees. It is no secret that Polish companies employed more manpower than was actually needed. For example there were usually 32-35 sea staff on board each vessel. When compared with west European standards, this implied around 30% overcapacity. The same problems also affected the numbers of people working ashore.

Another problem which needed to be overcome was where to place orders for new ships. Polish shipyards were no longer interested in building for Polish shipowners. The government support for exporting companies created a situation in which nobody was really interested in producing for the domestic market. The taxation system did not even support companies which were prepared to pay 100% in free currency.

As well as Polish domestic problems, there were a number which affected the international market. There appeared to be a real and urgent need to create an international forum for businessmen representing all European countries. Existing organisations, such as the International Maritime Organisation, the International Chamber of Commerce, UNCTAD and many others were concentrating their efforts on either general problems or very particular areas such as maritime fraud. The new forum could have promoted discussion on the following objectives:

-work to strengthen cooperation between east and west business, between government and the private sector, as a key to effective promotion of shipping;

-promotion of international standards that would positively influence government policy for shipping;

-formulation of solutions to practical problems facing shipping and related transport modes;

-organisation of meetings to tighten personal relations between businessmen from both sides of Europe.

Conclusions

Recapitulating, this short paper, the following remarks should be noted:

1   Shipowners from Poland were as prepared as could be expected in 1991, for the free market mechanism, which was being developed in Poland.

2   There is no doubt that all companies in Poland, and unfortunately this included shipowners as well, lacked new methods of management and needed to develop more effective marketing techniques. POL needed to

develop multimodal shipments in all services and not only on the North Atlantic trade.

3   Taking into consideration the poor experience of the CMEA initiatives to create joint ventures, and the concentration of capital in world shipping, there was a clear necessity to create new forms of cooperation between east and west European shipowners.

The place of Polish seaports in the Baltic Sea basin

Konrad Misztal
Institute of Maritime Transport and Seaborne Trade
University of Gdansk

Abstract

This short paper looks at the role and activities of Polish seaports in the new environment since the economic changes of the 1980s and 1990s.

Introduction

Political and economic changes in central and eastern Europe, along with a steady process of economic integration in western Europe, have created new external operating conditions for Polish ports. Previously, Polish ports operated in a monopolistic transport and economic environment, and hence they were not forced to compete for Polish foreign trade cargoes amongst themselves or with foreign ports. Moreover, movement of transit cargo from the former Czechoslovakia and Hungary, as members of the Council for Mutual Economic Assistance (CMEA), were mostly determined for political rather than economic reasons.

The new political and economic system in central and eastern Europe has changed the hinterland of Polish seaports, which are now determined by economic criteria. Due to these factors, the domestic and transit hinterlands of Polish seaports have become potential hinterlands for foreign port operators.

Seaport transition

The domestic hinterland of Polish seaports became international during the course of Poland's commercial liberalisation and the development of free exchange of commodities and services. As a consequence, monopolies in international trade and transport services were abolished and competition opened up for the Polish foreign trade cargo - most significantly to German ports in north Europe (Bremen and Hamburg), and the Adriatic ports in south Europe (Rijeka and Trieste). Hinterlands which once belonged to Polish seaports are being increasingly taken over by foreign land operators. On the other hand, Polish foreign trade has increased its interest in utilising foreign ports (competitive to the Polish ones) as a result of the abolition of state monopolies in foreign trade. It means that Polish importers and exporters will take into account only economic factors when choosing ports for their cargo. With a view to these pressing economic aspects, foreign ports may prove more profitable than Polish ones. The concept of free cargo and service movements, existing in the European economic region, is highly conducive to such a situation.

There have been notable territorial changes in the hinterlands of Polish seaports. The share of typical transit cargoes (from the Czech Republic, Slovakia and Hungary) in the total turnover of Polish ports is steadily diminishing. These countries, as well as Poland, have increased their cargo exchange with the European Union countries using mainly land transportation. Moreover, the commodities of these countries are increasingly being handled by German ports which benefit from a more favourable location in terms of shipping routes, than their Polish competitors. In addition, these ports generally offer a wider range of better quality services. However, there are some possibilities of attracting transit cargo to Polish seaports (particularly Gdansk and Gdynia) from Belorussia, north west Ukraine, and from the Baltic countries and the Kalingrad region of Russia, if only on a limited scale. In turn, the western hinterland is opening out to the eastern regions of Germany including the Berlin agglomeration, which could bring cargo transported in the Baltic region, to the port of Szczecin/Swinoujscie.

Territorial changes in the hinterlands of Polish ports are also occurring due to the development of transport infrastructure around Poland. This predominantly road infrastructure takes over more and more transit cargoes which passed through Poland previously. New east-west transport connections have proved disadvantageous to Polish ports particularly the development of new highways.

At the same time, Polish foreign trade has undergone a serious transformation regarding its directions and the use it makes of infrastructure. In recent years, there has been a rapid growth of cargo exchange between Poland and the west European countries, especially with European Union members, whilst the trade with former Communist countries is diminishing. This process is promoted by the agreement on the association of Poland to the European Union. In 1993, commodities imported from EU members amounted to 58% of total Polish imports whilst the share of goods exported to the EU amounted to 63% of Polish exports. Germany has become the most important trade partner for Poland. Cargo turnover with Germany reached 32% of Poland's total foreign turnover in 1993. With a 49% share of imports and 58% share of exports, Germany carries out more trade with Poland than any other EU member (1).

Accession of Poland to the European Union, which will require deep rooted changes in the Polish economy (leading to diminution of the dominant position maintained by primary industry, in favour of manufacturing and even service industry) brings about several changes in the structure of Polish foreign trade. At present highly manufactured goods dominate the structure of Polish imports from the European Union. The share of manufactured commodities in Polish exports to the EU is also growing. Such commodities tend to gravitate towards land transport modes. This has caused a decrease in Polish maritime trade (regarding general cargo) which may have an unfavourable impact upon the volume of transhipments in Polish seaports. In addition, alternative transportation routes and modes (away from rail and inland waterway) are becoming more competitive to the Polish ports.

It is evident from the trends noted above, that Polish seaports are operating in a transportation market which is competitive in every respect. Competition with foreign ports, which previously only concerned transit cargoes, has now also arisen in foreign trade. Moreover, land transport (most notably multimodal transport) is becoming more and more competitive with Polish seaports. In this situation, Polish seaports face the necessity of having to re-assert their position in international maritime transport and particularly in the Baltic Sea region.

The south eastern Baltic Sea region, where all Polish ports are situated, was politically and economically monopolised until 1989. Several limitations were imposed upon transport between the south eastern Baltic countries (members of the Communist bloc) and the north western Baltic countries. All socialist countries enforced a rule under which foreign trade could use only domestic ports in trade relations with foreign countries. Wider attraction of foreign cargoes to the home ports was impossible due to political reasons and as a result it was possible to observe a serious lack of connections and cooperation between the Baltic ports.

Changes which are taking place in the Baltic Sea region, create new possibilities for port operations and development. With a view to Polish ports, these possibilities depend on such factors as: geographic location, efficiency of transport links between the hinterland and foreland, land distribution systems and quality and prices of port services.

The location of Polish ports seriously limits their chances in the competitive transport market of the Baltic Sea region. Their location is peripheral to the main ocean shipping routes and to the European industrial regions. Hence, for several cargoes the economic and time distances are unfavourable. As a consequence, Polish ports will undoubtedly never reach a position of logistic and distribution centres on a European scale as the base ports for the European shipping and centres for cargo concentration for the European continent.

A steady concentration of ocean trade in several base ports (so called 'seaport polarisation') has led these Baltic ports to serve as regional and feeder ports, which supply cargo to the base ports. Large, west European ports such as Hamburg, Bremen, Rotterdam and Antwerp operate as the base ports for Baltic ocean trade (mainly containers).

The only port which has kept its oceanic position is the port in Gothenburg. The other Baltic ports became the regional ones, adapting themselves to the new role by constructing specialised ro-ro berths, terminals for feeder lines and regular Baltic lines. In the light of this tendency, Polish ports may look for development possibilities in re-opening Baltic shipping connections with Swedish, Finnish and Dutch ports, along with opening new shipping lines to St Petersburg and to the ports of Latvia, Lithuania and Estonia.

New perspectives for Polish ports may arise from the enlargement of the transit hinterland for Gdansk and Gdynia ports (including the transit markets of Belorussia, north west Ukraine and the Baltic countries - Lithuania and Latvia) and for the ports of Szczecin and Swinoujscie (embracing north east Germany with the ports of the Berlin agglomeration). In this new hinterland system, Polish ports may play the role of the main agent in maritime export of such cargo as iron ore and coal from the Ukraine, fertilisers from Belorussia and oil imports to Lithuania, Latvia, Estonia and the former GDR. Poland operates the only deep water base for liquid cargo on the Baltic in the Northern port in Gdansk which can accommodate the biggest tankers that can enter the Baltic Sea (vessels of 150,000 capacity). That terminal is also connected by pipeline to Schwedt (Germany). There are still some possibilities in the sphere of transhipment and storage services

- Polish ports may operate as transhipment ports for these Baltic countries (Lithuania, Latvia and Estonia) which have not sufficient capacity for handling containers, ro-ro units and other special cargo.

For Polish ports the success in attracting transit cargo will depend on an efficient system of transport connections to the whole economic hinterland and on effective port connections to the land distribution system.

The railway transport infrastructure corresponds with the majority of European standards. Both port complexes, Gdansk-Gdynia and Szczecin-Swinoujscie are connected with domestic and transit hinterland by two meridian railway lines, linked to the main railway system of central and southern Europe (although some difficulties may occur on borders). However, the access to the road system is more difficult (especially within the territory of port cities and in their direct hinterland). Among other factors unfavourable to Polish ports, one may mention the underdeveloped motorway system, the lack of ring roads around the towns, low traffic capacity on the borders and low internationalisation of Polish roads running in meridian and latitudinal directions.

Incorporation of Poland into the European north-south transport corridors provides Poland a chance of attracting cargo and passengers to national ports. The favourable location of Poland in that system may be conducive to the development of sea-land transit on the north-south route (using sea routes linking Polish ports with Scandinavian countries).

The Pollink system, embracing a new Baltic transport chain (a ferry connection between ports of Stockholm and Gdansk agglomerations) is very important for the Polish transport corridor. Pollink is the shortest ferry-railway and ferry-road connection between Finland and south-east Sweden and southern Europe (via the ports of Gdansk and Gdynia). The Trans-European Railway (TER) and Trans European Motorway (TEM) constitute the land chains of the corridor. Within the TEM and TER projects it is planned to construct modern railway and road connections between Scandinavia and central-eastern European countries, via the ports of Szczecin and Gdansk, and with the Mediterranean countries. Development of these corridors will influence both cargo and passenger movements in Scandinavia - south Europe-Near East directions. In this corridor, Poland is considered to be a natural transit route. It will result in the growth of multimodal transportation, ro-ro and ferry passenger shipping and international tourism, thus influencing the development of passenger movements. To take advantage of these opportunities, Poland should create proper conditions for taking over these cargo and passenger movements, mostly through investment in ports and through the development of transport infrastructure in the hinterland. In such a situation ferry shipping will gain a more important position. The share of Polish ferry shipping in serving this demand until now, has been rather small. Regarding total transportation on the Baltic Sea in 1990, the share of Polish ferries amounted to only 1% in passenger transport, 2% in passenger cars and caravans, 0.9% in buses, 5% in trucks and trailers, 4% in railway carriages and 4% in cargoes transported using the piggy-back system. The following years have not brought many changes. This low participation of Polish interests in the ferry transportation of the Baltic is a result of the underdeveloped transport system within Poland, and from the small scale of Polish ferry shipping./

The geographic location of Polish seaports places them in a strong position for potential development into important transit ports in the north-south transport system in the Baltic Sea basin. Political and economic changes which occurred in the Baltic Sea region are conducive to cooperation not only between regional seaports but also between their cities. The establishment of the Union of Baltic Cities (with its Secretariat in Gdansk) may serve as evidence to that. In the light of the above mentioned facts, the position of Polish seaports in the Baltic system, would seem to consist of:

1   Maintaining a dominant place in handling Polish foreign trade cargoes, both general and bulk;

2   performing the function of feeder ports for containerised cargo - it requires the development of ro-ro berths and ferry terminals which will serve feeder lines to base ports in north-west Europe, along with opening new connections to ports in the Baltic Sea region;

3   performing the function of transit ports in the system of European north south transport corridors, passing from Scandinavia via Polish seaports to southern Europe, and further to the Near East - thus taking over cargo and passenger movements in that direction;

4   performing the function of transhipment ports for the Baltic States (Lithuania, Latvia and Estonia) whose transhipment capacity is not sufficient for handling containerised, ro-ro and other specialised cargo;

5   performing the function of an oil transhipment centre based on the only deep water specialised base in that region which can accommodate the largest tankers entering the Baltic Sea;

6   performing the function of a main centre for handling foreign trade of Belorussia and north west Ukraine (the ports in Gdansk and Gdynia), and also for commodities from the eastern German region flowing towards the Baltic (the ports in Szczecin and Swinoujscie).

Liability, conventions, classification societies and safety in the Baltic - a case study of the Estonia

Chris Dent and Michael Roe
Institute of Marine Studies
University of Plymouth

Abstract

As the carrying capacity of passenger Ro' Ro' ferries has continued to grow, certain established shipping practices and legislation may have been slow to keep up. As a result, it is possible that two particular areas have fallen so far behind that they could actually encourage the operation of substandard ships; classification societies and limitation of liability Conventions. This paper examines the current role and structure of these two important bodies to identify where any shortfalls may be.

The main problem with limitation Conventions is the possibility that levels of limitation are set too low, and that insurers can deviate from the Articles of the Convention as and when it suits them. The fact that levels of liability are too low may remove much of the incentive for shipowners to spend extra money on safety. Insurers are also allowed to exercise so much flexibility as to the amount of the compensation offered, that this may further remove the shipowners' incentive to improve safety. With respect to classification societies, the service that they currently provide to shipping may be marginalised and insufficient to eradicate the operation of poor quality ships. It is also possible that market forces serve to keep this status quo. In addition, classification societies are virtually 'untouchable' when it comes to liability for their acts or omissions, and as such this may increase the problems mentioned. To support and illustrate these arguments, developments following the recent Ro' Ro' ferry accident 'Estonia' are analysed and discussed.

The ultimate conclusion is that limitation of liability Conventions, and classification societies are in need of restructuring in particular areas. This should be carried out in conjunction with structural changes to the actual design of Ro' Ro' ferries to help increase the levels of safety in shipping, and so that any further loop holes are removed.

Introduction

During that last ten years, Roll-on Roll-off (Ro' Ro') passenger ferries have undergone many changes in an effort to make them more cost effective and competitive to operate. Included among these changes has been a substantial increase in size and carrying capacity, and the ability for faster turn-around times. The increase in carrying capacity has meant that a modern ferry may be carrying up to 3,000 passengers at one time.

From a practical point of view, there exists the possibility that one of these ferries may be involved in an incident that results in loss of life or personal injury to passengers. Following such an event the shipowner, subject to the terms of the particular Convention governing such events, may be allowed to limit the extent of his financial liability to a fixed amount. This practice is well established and there is a strong argument for its existence, the main justification being that it allows shipowners to assess the extent of their potential losses, and insure against them as appropriate. However, there is a question of whether or not the existence of limitation of liability Conventions could have any significant relationship to ferry safety. In addition, the current role of classification societies and their certification procedure may also have safety ramifications. These are questions which have not received proper attention. It is the broad aim of this paper to ascertain:

1   If current limitation of liability Conventions have any causal relationship to the relative safety of Ro' Ro' passenger vessels, and if the application of these Conventions may have contributed to the creation of a substandard level of safety in the Ro' Ro' passenger ferry sector.

2   If classification procedures are adequate enough to help eradicate substandard ships.

In order to achieve its primary aim, this paper will analyse the process of compensation for claims of personal injury and loss of life following a ferry disaster, and see how this process is affected by limitation Conventions. Additionally the paper will examine some of the potential effects of the limitation Conventions on ship operators, shipowners, passengers, and most prominently, classification societies. This should help to determine if there is any evidence to suggest that current liability limitation provisions have safety implications with respect to Ro' Ro' passenger vessels. To achieve an up-to-date perspective in this field, the paper will concentrate on the relatively recent 'Estonia' case.

Background

On the 28th September 1994, the Ro' Ro' passenger ferry 'Estonia' capsized and sank in the Baltic Sea with the loss of 852 lives. The 21,794 Gt. Estonia (formerly the Viking Sally, Silja Star and Wasa King) was built at the Meyer shipyard in Papenburg, Germany in 1980. She was purchased from Wasa Line (a subsidiary of Silja Line) in January 1993 by Estline, a joint venture between the state owned 'Estonian Shipping Company' and 'Nordstrum & Thulin' of Sweden (Lloyds List, 1994, p. 1). The Estonia was purchased to replace the smaller Nord Estonia in order to satisfy the increasing demand on the busy Tallinn to Stockholm route.

The Estonia operated the 15 hour crossing twice weekly on a scheduled service under the Estonian flag, and was entered with the Oslo based P&I Club Assuranceforeningen Skuld, (Skuld) for all passenger liabilities. The ship's hull and machinery was covered for $48 million and a $12 million increased value policy was added, bringing the vessel's hull and machinery insurance up to $60 million. The Estonia had an A/Amax figure of 95 per cent, the A/Amax figure having been designed to assess the likelihood of a ship surviving a collision (the present required A/Amax figure for ferries operating in most of northern Europe is 70%, however this will be upgraded to 95% in 1999). The Estonia's classification society was Bureau Veritas of France. She was certified to carry 2,000 passengers and passed her most recent annual survey in August 1994. The design of Estonia's bow loading door is referred to as a 'visor' type bow door, and is relatively common among Ro' Ro' ferries as it facilitates a quick turnaround time. Upon arriving up at the terminal, the bow of the ferry is hydraulically raised. Once the bow is in the upright position, the inner door can be lowered in order to act as the loading ramp, thus providing vehicles with access onto and off the vessel's decks. The ramp, when in its vertical seagoing position, performs the task of a water-tight bulkhead, which is vital to the safety of the vessel and designed to counter any potential threat of water leaking onto the vehicle decks through the bow door.

Since the sinking, subsequent testimonies by survivors and inspections of the wreck by independent accident investigators, have concluded that the cause of the sinking was due to three integral locking devices on the bow door simultaneously failing rendering the bow door loose; a chain of events then followed this initial failure. Strong winds gusting at about 25 metres per second, continuously pounded waves of up to 10 metres in height against the now loose visor door causing uncontrollable movement. The bow door then in turn smashed against the inner ramp door (prior to the bow being eventually ripped off). The effect of this was to crack open the inner ramp door, thus allowing water to enter onto the car deck. The ingress of water created a 'free flow effect' which altered the vessel's centres of gravity and buoyancy, leading to a loss of stability and eventual capsize (Lloyds List, 1994, p. 14).

The high proportion of deaths in the sinking of the Estonia have been attributed not only to the faulty bow door and the ingress of water, but also to other factors. For example, many people at the time of the incident (about midnight) were asleep or in their cabins. There was no power or lighting on the vessel as the ship had experienced a blackout shortly after the initial ingress of water; the evacuation of the vessel in a heavy list and darkness was therefore very difficult to organise. The temperature of the water was very cold, about 10 degrees Celsius (Lloyds List, 1994, p. 15), thus reducing the survival time of people who had actually managed to escape the sinking vessel. it is also questionable whether the crew and passengers were made aware of the situation in sufficient time to allow for an adequate evacuation, and whether the distress signal (Mayday) was broadcast as soon as it should have been. The Estonia sank in international waters at an estimated 0040 hours; within 35 minutes of water entering the deck. The Estonia had on board a total of 989 people; 803 passengers and 186 members of crew - 852 people died and there were 137 survivors.

Establishing the legal framework

Following the sinking, the method of recourse for the survivors and families of the injured and deceased was to turn to Skuld who had accepted the risks for loss of life and personal injury on behalf of the vessel. In order to cope with the large number of enquiries from concerned relatives in both Sweden and in Estonia, Skuld established temporary claims handling offices in Stockholm and Tallinn. These facilities initially offered interim so-called 'hardship payments' to those relatives who were in need of immediate financial assistance, and also provided updated information and reports to relatives and press about the names of the deceased so far and the status of survivors. As the search and rescue operations were gradually suspended and a clearer picture of what had taken place started to emerge, compensation procedures began to get underway. Support groups were established, the most far-reaching and prominent with backing from about 82% of those involved being the 'International Support Group'. This group was set up by a relative in order to integrate and join together the survivors and relatives and provide them with a unified voice. The support group began to communicate with Skuld and would be involved with and consulted in the eventual formation of the compensation offer. However, before Skuld could start to assess accurately the scale of the total payment and begin processing the compensation claims, several significant questions needed to be addressed in order to establish which liability regime and legal framework to work within. First, Skuld had to establish if any international Convention or national legislation on the limitation of liability could be applied to the personal injury and loss of life claims arising from the sinking. If a Convention was applicable then what were its provisions and scope of application?

Athens Convention on the Carriage of Passengers and their Luggage by Sea, 1974

One of the leading Conventions on the carriage of passengers at sea is the Athens Convention 1974. Its limitation regime under Article 7 (1), allows for 46,666* Special Drawing Rights (SDR) multiplied by the number of passengers actually carried. Neither Sweden nor Estonia had ratified this convention thus seemingly excluding its application in this case. Nevertheless application of the Athens Convention still raised some interesting legal issues. As mentioned, the State of Estonia had not ratified the Convention, but the USSR as Estonia's predecessor State had. However, the independence of Estonia in August 1991 served to nullify the USSR's prior ratification.

The fact that the Estonia sank in international waters, whose fishing grounds were claimed by Finland; and that the claimants covered a wide range of different nationalities also raised possible complications of application. Article 2 (i) of the Athens Convention clarifies these points and states that the Convention shall only apply to an international carriage if: (a) the ship is flying the flag of or is registered in a State Party to this Convention, or (b) the contract of carriage has been made in a State Party to this Convention, or (c) the place of departure or destination, according to the contract of carriage, is in a State Party to this Convention.

As has been illustrated, because of the non-ratification by Estonia and Sweden and because of Article 2 above; regardless of the position of the sinking and the varied nationalities of the claimants, the Athens Convention is not applicable in this case. Skuld were then forced to look elsewhere for limitation, and began to investigate the possibility of basing the compensation settlement on the Convention on Limitation of Liability for Maritime Claims 1976.

*   Subject to a 1990 protocol, ratification of which will set the limit at 175,000 SDR.

London Convention on the Limitation of Liability for Maritime Claims 1976

The (London) Convention on Limitation of Liability for Maritime Claims 1976 (CLLMC) was a more likely candidate for application. It was ratified by Sweden in 1984 and was incorporated into Swedish law on 1 December 1986 under the Swedish Damages Act, (also known as the Nordic Compensation Scheme). The CLLMC 1976 contains 23 Articles of Application. Those Articles most pertinent to this section of the paper are briefly summarised as follows:

Article 1 Persons entitled to limit

i)   Shipowners.
ii)   The term 'shipowner' includes the owner, charterer, manager and operator.
iv)   If any claims set out in Article 2 are made against any person for whose act, neglect or default the shipowner ...is responsible, such person shall be entitled to avail himself of the limitation of liability provided for in this Convention.
v)   The vessel herself.
vi)   An insurer of the vessel's liabilities in accordance with the rules of this Convention.

NB: The act of invoking limitation of liability shall not constitute an admission of liability.

Article 2 Claims subject to limitation

i)(a)   Subject to Articles 3 and 4: claims in respect of loss of life or personal injury shall be subject to limitation of liability.

Article 3 Claims expected from limitation

(e)   The rules of this Convention shall not apply to: claims by servants of the shipowner ...whose duties are connected with the ship ...including claims of their heirs or dependants.

Article 4 Conduct barring limitation

A person liable shall not be entitled to limit his liability if it is proved that the loss resulted from his personal act or omission, committed with the intent to cause such loss, or recklessly and with knowledge that such loss would probably result.

Article 7   The limit for passenger claims

i)   In respect of claims arising on any distinct occasion for loss of life or personal injury to passengers of a ship, the limit of liability shall be an amount of *46,666 Units of Account** multiplied by the number of passengers which the ship is authorised to carry according to the ship's certificate, *but not exceeding 25,000,000 Units of Account.*

Article 8   Unit of Account

i)   The Unit of Account referred to is the Special Drawing Right**(SDR). This shall then be converted into the national currency of the State in which limitation is sought.

Interpretation of the CLLMC 1976

Sweden has ratified the CLLMC, and it appears that the circumstances surrounding the sinking of the Estonia met fully the requirements set out in the Articles of the Convention. It would seem therefore, that in implementing the CLLMC one question needed to be answered in connection with Article 4, the question of 'conduct barring limitation'. The problem came down to whether or not the shipowners could be found to have been 'negligent' with respect to Article 4; if so then the shipowners' right to limit liability would be lost.

As is frequently the case surrounding incidents of this nature following thorough investigation, some degree of negligence can often be found (Leading Developments in International Marine Insurance, 1991). Under Scandinavian law for a shipowner to be held liable, all that needs to be shown is that somebody for whom the shipowner is responsible for has acted in a negligent manner (e.g., the master or crew). With the Estonia there are question marks over the actions of the master following his being made aware of the ingress of water, such as the length of time that passed

---

* Under Swedish law, the figure of 46,666 SDR has subsequently been increased to 100,000 SDR.
** The SDR is a unit of account whose value is based on market exchange rates and determined daily by the International Monetary Fund (IMF). The SDR is more popular and practical than its predecessor, the 'poincare franc' and is applied to virtually all Conventions dealing with liability limitation. The United States Dollar rate of the SDR as at 30 September 1994 was $1.46619.

before sending out a distress signal and alerting the passengers and crew. If the master had acted more expeditiously would the loss of life have been as high? This is a controversial point and is hard to answer with complete accuracy, however; sections of a leaked draft report undertaken by an independent investigative committee into the sinking appeared in Lloyds List 1994. Within the report were allegations that the master:

> ... was slow to warn passengers, crew and the Coast Guard of the impending danger ... it is doubtful that the passengers received any comprehensible warning at all.

Kaare Brandsjo, a member of the committee, implied that passengers and crew had little chance of getting into the lifeboats, and that lives would have been saved if the Finnish rescue services been immediately alerted (Lloyds List 1994, p. 10). This would seem to be backed up by the fact that loud bangs from the bow of the vessel were reported to the master by a crew member at 2340 hours, yet the crew were not alerted until 40 minutes later at 0020 hours. The first mayday signal was not transmitted until 0023 hours, the Estonia then sank at an estimated 0040 hours. The question then became whether or not the master's "personal act of omission, [was] committed with the intent to cause such loss, or recklessly and with knowledge that such loss would probably result", (as per Article 4). If so, it could have then provided the basis for the loss of the right to limit.

As far as Skuld were concerned however, the possible application of Article 4 and the potential loss of limitation did not pose too great a threat. For their side of the argument, the fact that the master was seemingly torpid in raising the alarm was not the reason for the bow door being ripped off in the first place; surely any issue of neglect therefore would fall squarely on the shoulders of either the shipbuilders for the faulty locks on the bow door, or the Classification Society for passing the door as safe; would it not be within expectations to expect a high death toll after the vessel has sustained such dramatic damage on the high seas. In addition, the master and his complement of officers "who were extremely qualified and held in very high regard within their profession" (Gunnar Bendreus) are believed to have gone down with the vessel, and obviously therefore can not be posed questions about the reasons for their actions. Because this issue has become so blurred, it would take a large amount of money and time to be proved either way in court. The possibility of the survivors group taking legal action over this particularly contentious matter was remote, nevertheless it was a possibility and it may have influenced the future decisions of the P&I Club when it came to the formation of the compensation offer. Consequently, Skuld decided that the CLLMC 1976 was to be used to form the basis of the compensation package.

Another interesting point about the CLLMC is that Article 3(e) excludes employees, servants or their relatives from claiming for compensation under the same scheme as the passengers. Any claims from employees and their relatives are therefore dealt with as per the contract of employment, and not according to the CLLMC.

As previously mentioned, under Article 7 of the CLLMC the limits of liability were set out as 46,666 SDR. Under Swedish Law this has since been increased to 100,000 SDR multiplied by the number of passengers that the vessel is authorised to carry. The Estonia was certified to carry a maximum of 2,000 passengers:

$$\therefore \quad 100,000 * 2,000 = 200,000,000 \text{ SDR}$$

Article 7 however, also states that there is an overall per ship limit to liability of 25,000,000 SDR. Applying the United States Dollar rate of the SDR as at 30 September 1994 of $1.46619:

$$\therefore \quad 25,000,000 * 1.46619 = \$36,654,750$$

Therefore the claims for personal injury and loss of life, for the victims and relatives of the Estonia would be based on the rules of the CLLMC, and were subject to an overall limit of $36.7 million.

The compensation offer

The offer was based on the CLLMC but in many cases dictated according to the personal circumstances of the claimants, for example, the salary and age of the deceased and the proximity of the relationship at the time of the accident. In order for the offer to be binding, Skuld required that at least 90% of the claimants had to accept it. If the offer was not met with the required support of 90% then Skuld were entitled to revoke the offer. However, Skuld would be entitled to maintain the offer to those claimants who agreed to the terms. Upon acceptance of the offer, payments to claimants who were residents of a Scandinavian country (i.e., Sweden, Norway, Finland or Denmark) at the time of the incident would be awarded in Swedish Kroner (SEK). Claimants domiciled elsewhere were entitled to elect either, SEK, the Estonian Kroon (EEK), or United States Dollars (USD) as their chosen currency. Furthermore, Estonian claimants would be entitled only to 65% of the amounts on offer to Scandinavian and other nationality claimants; this was to allow exchange rates and the lower cost of living to be accounted for. Where a claimant falls into more than one group, compensation is offered in all groups of which that claimant becomes a member. The amounts were offered in SEK but for this paper have been converted to USD to provide easier understanding and continuity.

Group 1

Claimants who at the time of the accident were married to or living in marriage-like relationships with deceased persons.

Compensation to the group -

(a) $33,500

(b)   An amount corresponding to the annual income of the deceased (excluding income from capital), multiplied by 1.8. This amount shall not be less than $20,000 and not more than $135,000.

(c)   If the claimant had a child by the deceased, or had custody of children of the claimants own, aged under 19; $230 multiplied by the total number of months, which at the time of the accident remained to pass before each child attained the age of 19.

Group 2

Children under the age of 19 who were left without parents due to the accident (or if only one parent, whose only parent was lost in the accident).

Compensation to the group -

Claimants belonging to this group are offered compensation equalling the sum total of compensation stated in (a) and (b) below.

(a) $70,000.

(b) $535, multiplied by the number of months which remained a pass at the time of the accident before the child attains the age of 19.

Group 3

Children under 19 who lost a parent or other person married to or living in a marriage-like relationship with the child's custodial parent, in the accident.

Compensation to the group-

Claimants belonging to this group are offered compensation equalling the sum total of compensation stated in (a) and (b) below.

(a) $35,000.

(b) $110, multiplied by the number of months which at the time of the accident remained to pass before the child attains the age of 19.

Group 4A

Children aged 19 but under 22 who lost one or both parents or another custodian in the accident.

Compensation to the group -

Claimants belonging to this group are offered compensation equalling the sum total offered in (a), (b) and (c) below.

(a) $10,000 per deceased person but not less than $20,000 if no claimant connected with the child receives compensation in group 1 or 5.

(b)   If any claimant connected with the child receives compensation in group 1 or 5: $335, multiplied by the number of months which at the time of the accident remained to pass before the child attains the age of 22.

(c)   If no claimant connected with the child received compensation in group 1 or 5: $670, multiplied by the number of months which at the time of the accident remained to pass before the child attains the age of 22.

Group 4B

Children aged 19 but under 25 who in the accident lost one or both parents or another custodian.

Compensation to the group -

(a) $4,000.

Group 5

Parents who lost a person with whom they had children at the time of the accident and who are not receiving compensation in Group 1.

Compensation to the group -

Claimants belonging to this group are offered compensation equalling the sum total of compensation stated in (a) and (b) below.

(a) $10,000.

(b)   125 per cent of the highest monthly contribution towards the children's support which was agreed on, or determined before the incident, or which would have been awarded by a competent court/public authority. Not to be less than $335 per month for each month remaining to pass before the child attains the age of 19.

Group 6

Claimants, other than those included in group 1, 2, 3, 4 and 5, above who were supported by a deceased person.

Compensation to the group -

(a)   125 per cent of compensation calculated according to Swedish law, for the loss of support, with deduction for the amounts stated in Group 4, points (a), (b) and (c), and Group 5, point (a).

Group 7

Parents or other custodians of a deceased person, and children aged 22 or over who lost parents or other custodian.

Compensation to the group -

(a) $10,000 per deceased person.

Group 8

Relatives of deceased persons in cases where no compensation is paid in connection with a deceased person in Groups 1 - 5 and/or 7, above.

Compensation to the group-

(a) $5,360 per deceased person.

Group 9

Claimants who were connected with a deceased person and who have incurred a loss other than loss of support.

Compensation to the group -

(a)   Compensation as provided in Swedish law is offered for damage, expenses and losses referred to in Group 9 above. If, however, a claimant receives compensation in Groups 1 - 8, a deduction of $5,360 shall be made from the compensation payable in this group.

(b)   For persistent discomfort and loss caused by psychological damage resulting from the accident, compensation as provided in Swedish law is offered with the addition of 25% of the compensation thus calculated.

Group 10

Survivors

(a)   Survivors will receive $20,000 as compensation for pain and suffering.

(b)   In the event of a survivor subsequently dying from injuries sustained as a result of the accident, compensation is offered in accordance with that outlined in the above-mentioned groups.

(c)   For persistent discomfort and loss including damage other than loss of support, and caused by mental or physical injury sustained as a result of the accident, compensation is offered as provided by Swedish law with the addition of 25% of the compensation thus calculated. If a survivor has received compensation under Group 10, point (a), a deduction of $4,000 shall be made.

The offer above sets out the amounts of money that certain groups of claimants are entitled to receive in respect of compensation from the P&I Club Skuld for passenger liabilities. Other salient points applying to the general offer were written into the compensation document, and are summarised below:

- Interest on amounts payable will accrue from 1 December 1994 until payment is effected.

- In cases of fatalities, Skuld agreed to meet the costs of funeral expenses, and other reasonable expenses entailed by death.

- Skuld is entitled to deduct any previous payments made, such as hardship payments.

- Neither the shipping company nor Skuld are deemed to have accepted any liability towards the claimants through this offer.

- Acceptance of the offer means that an agreement on full and final economic settlement has been concluded between the parties concerning all the claimants claim.

- By accepting the offer, no further compensation claims can be lodged against the Shipping Company or Skuld, or any other party insured with Skuld, (however this does not discount the possibility of suing some other third party in damages).

- No deductions will be made from claimants who have received payments made under personal insurance.

- Claims under Groups 9 and 10 will become time-barred on 28 September 1999 unless legal action has been brought prior to that data.

- Interpretation and implementation of the offer is subject to Swedish law.

Analysis of the compensation offer

A total compensation package of $75 million was formally accepted by more than the required 90% of about 3,000 claimants on 21 March 1995. The award amounted to more than double the per ship limitation of $36.7 million as prescribed under Article 7 (i) of the CLLMC. It is therefore necessary to analyse the structure of the offer and examine the reasons for exceeding that limitation. The procedure of separating claimants into ten almost identical groups was used by Skuld in the Scandinavian Star incident of 1990 where 159 people lost their lives, as was the requirement of at least 90% approval of the offer. However, another similarity with other settlements of this kind was that the final payout was more than the P&I Club were actually obliged to pay.

The reason for the structure of the offer and exceeding the liability regime of the CLLMC was twofold. First, the overall per ship limitation creates a potentially unfortunate anomaly in that the greater the loss of life, the less compensation will be received by each claimant. By way of an example using the figures from earlier in this paper, if the overall ship limit of liability is 25 million SDR, and a ship was carrying 2,000 passengers, then a maximum of only 12,500 SDR would be available for the survivors and families of each fatality.

In terms of compensation, calculated with the USD rate of the SDR as at 30 September 1994, this would equate to about $18,327. Naturally therefore, the large number of claimants who registered for compensation and their relationship to the deceased served to push the figures up. Second, and perhaps most importantly, Skuld stood to make financial savings by dealing with the lawyers who represented the whole 'group' as opposed to dealing with individual lawyers for each claimant. Therefore it was definitely in their interests to keep the group together. If a large proportion of the group did not approve the offer and became fragmented, then jurisdiction would have been spread throughout Estonia, Sweden and the other nations where claimants were domiciled. Pursuing individual claims would have created substantially increased legal costs, extra administration costs and it would take much longer to finalise the payments, leading to greater interest payments on outstanding claims. Therefore, in order to keep the group together, it was important for Skuld to make the offer tempting to the majority of claimants. The second reason bears some resemblance to the term known as the 'Mid-Atlantic Solution'.

The Mid-Atlantic solution

The so-called Mid-Atlantic solution is a strategy used by defence lawyers to deter claimants from going to court in the USA. It usually occurs in cases where the event in question happened outside of the USA, yet there remains the possibility of legal action being brought by the claimants in the USA through some American link; this may be the case for example if there were American crew members or passengers. In respect of mass tort claims, the USA is (from the claimants point of view), a very good forum of law for the following important reasons.

1   American law does not look favourably upon shipowners, insurers or P&I Clubs who wish to exercise the right to limitation of liability, as it is held to be *"against the constitution and the common good"*.

2   Unlike Scandinavian law the burden of proof rests with the owner to prove that he has not been negligent, rather than the claimants trying to prove that he has been negligent.

3   If the owner or his employees are found to have been negligent or reckless, the court may (and usually will) impose punitive damages on the shipowner. Punitive damages may add up to as much as the amount offered as compensation itself, thereby doubling the amount awarded.

4   Any injured party, no matter how 'non-material' their injuries may appear are entitled to a jury trial; this includes a strong emphasis on many intangible virtues such as 'loss of feelings', 'loss of quality of life', and 'loss of sexual pleasure'. These awards can be substantial, for example, in a recent settlement made to a widow of one of the victims of the Lockerbie aircraft bombing, $19 million was awarded. This included $9 million for the loss of her husband's career and financial support, $5 million for loss of companionship and $5 million in interest payments (Lloyds List, 1995, p. 10).

5   Juries are made up of 'ordinary people', whom defence lawyers believe are easily influenced by harrowing accounts of the events given by the claimants. The jury are allowed to hear subjective arguments, they decide on the matter of the owners' negligence, and it is they, not the judge, who decide on the amount of compensation to be offered (Leading Developments in International Marine Insurance, 1991, pp. 79-81).

The Mid-Atlantic solution is so-called because it applies the process of 'tempting' claimants away from American jurisdiction by offering them swift payment of amounts in excess of those prescribed by the limitation conventions, yet below those that would be available through the USA courts. This then provides a settlement which is not as large as one which would be made by an American court, but is more than would have been offered under Scandinavian law. Clearly it is understood why a defence lawyer in a mass tort action would wish to avoid the USA as a forum of law, and why this 'solution' was developed. Although in the particular case of the Estonia it appeared unlikely that a strong enough connection could be made with America in order to instigate legal proceedings there, this was a risk that Skuld would be unlikely to take, and it is most probable that Skuld kept a very close eye on any developments with this situation. For this reason and those given above, it is believed that Skuld decided to apply the basic formula of the Mid-Atlantic solution to the compensation offer, and double the extent of their limit of liability from $36.7 million to $75 million.

Possible effects of conventions and P&I Club flexibility on safety

So far we have seen that regardless of the relevant convention in place, P&I Clubs have almost complete control over the amount of compensation to be offered to claimants. This flexibility on the side of the P&I Clubs may seem fair enough as they hold the purse strings after all, but this then raises the question; what is the purpose of the convention if it is not to set the level of compensation and enforce it? The answer to the question seems to be that many of the conventions (in this case the CLLMC) fulfil the roles of purely advisory documents, whose objective is merely to lay down the guidelines for the payment of compensation. The issue now is whether this is a positive development for claimants of a maritime disaster, or whether it could have negative effects on various passenger safety issues.

It is true that the flexibility afforded to the P&I Clubs can have benefits to many claimants, and the middle ground afforded by the mid-Atlantic solution does have it's meritorious points. As discussed, in the particular case of the Estonia the amounts awarded were much higher than would be allowed under the convention. Claimants naturally prefer to receive higher awards as it can help them feel that sufficient justice has been served upon the guilty party, compensation can also go some way to reducing feelings of loss and suffering, and there are also obvious financial benefits (Leading Developments in International Marine Insurance, 1991, pp. 79-81). It is possible, however, that this practice may have created a 'hidden', long term damaging effect on passenger safety. The main problem is that the limits of liability as they are set out in various conventions are too low, and they provide too much flexibility for the P&I Clubs. Therefore, shipowners have little incentive to spend money on improving safety standards because their potential losses are not proportionately that high. Also, any losses suffered are usually covered with a P&I Club who can 'spread' the risk to the extent that no significant financial effect is felt by anyone in the chain.

If limits were set higher, P&I Clubs would be forced to exert pressure on certain shipowners to run safer ships. The Clubs would then have to impose restrictions on certain vessels which did not meet a prescribed high level of safety. Any substandard vessels would have to meet the new specifications or face loss of cover, and any resulting loss of business. Another aspect of this would be that P&I Clubs would put extra pressure on classification societies to provide a better service, and perhaps to open the door to classification society liability.

Classification societies

At present, classification societies seemingly enjoy an almost *"unique position of complete freedom from legal liability for any and all of its actions"* (Fairplay, 1995, pp. 3-4, 9, 28-29). This autonomous freedom is quite startling when the human stakes involved with large Ro' Ro' ferries are considered. Furthermore, if the certificate of a vessels class is not a statement of fact, and a guarantee of seaworthiness then what is its purpose? In a recent case, the *Nicholas H (1992) 2 Lloyds Rep 481*, the court upheld previous similar decisions that:

> The purpose of the classification certificate was not to guarantee safety, but merely to permit the shipowner to take advantage of the insurance rates available to a classed vessel.

The fact that classification societies (by necessity) are becoming increasingly exposed to free market forces, and that this may make their job of enforcing safety standards much more difficult, may lead some to argue that classification societies are moving in the wrong direction. In an effort to reverse this trend perhaps the situation could be created whereby; following a maritime incident and a full investigation of the causes, a clear chain of liability could be established, starting at the ship builders yard, and ending with the operators. Classification societies would be included in this chain, and where appropriate, could be held fully, or partly, responsible for their acts or omissions. This so-called chain would be capable of deducing where liability rests between all the parties involved in the operation of the vessel, resulting in drastic improvements in standards of classification. Another necessary change would involve creating a clearer link between the classification societies and their obligation to provide a 'duty of care' to third parties, such as cargo owners, charterers, victims of pollution and passengers. This would require re-wording of the terms and conditions found on the back of the classification certificate (Appendix C). Also, the scope of the surveys carried out by classification societies should be expanded to include checks on lifesaving equipment, the proficiency of cargo loading methods, and the competency of crews. At first, as with many new ideas, this suggestion may appear inappropriate or too radical. For example, many shipowners may not be initially happy with the heightened standards and the extra costs involved. However, changes such as these are needed in order to provide a solid base on which to build up the Ro' Ro' ferry sector's image, and in order to compete with other modes of transportation, (principally air and rail/tunnel). While these methods may seem somewhat drastic to some, they only appear so because of the relatively slow pace at which changes in the shipping industry are brought about, and because shipping in general is behind the field in terms of practical, relevant and workable safety legislation.

Practical reasons for change

Two central legislative flaws which therefore may have the propensity to promote substandard ferries and ferry operations as discussed, have been identified as follows:

i)   Limits of liability are set too low to be an effective deterrent to shipowners who operate potentially dangerous vessels.
ii)   Classification societies shoulder limited responsibility for their acts or omissions when placing vessels in class.

In order for change to be brought about rapidly, shipowners, operators, insurers and legislators must become actively involved. The obvious and most important reason to implement increased safety measures on Ro' Ro' ferries is to save lives. Table 1 illustrates the argument that in certain conditions the stability of the Ro' Ro' concept is suspect. In addition, the table challenges claims that incidents such as the Estonia are merely 'one offs' or 'freak accidents'.

Surely the biggest incentive for shipowners to push for changes in safety standards, is that every disaster costs them millions in lost revenue through public fear and bad publicity following an accident. The loss of passenger confidence and revenue is not only borne by the operator involved with the incident but is usually seen across the board of ferry operators, thereby depressing a large proportion of the ferry sector and affecting many different markets and operators all at the same time. The actual cost of the loss in revenue and the damage caused by future passenger rejection is virtually impossible to calculate, yet figures from 1994 (see Table 2) show that six Baltic ferry operators experienced a decline in passenger numbers following, and as a direct result of the Estonia incident. In addition to reductions in passenger numbers and a loss of revenue, there is also medium to long term negative publicity following such an incident. In order to counter any negative publicity, operators are often forced to cut ticket prices to try and entice customers back, they also face an increase in their marketing expenditure, thus resulting in a further drop in revenue. There are other financial considerations such as repairing any damage to a vessel, or in cases of total loss, the cost of purchasing a new vessel to replace the previous one. Salvage costs may also be necessary.

Table 1
Major Ro' Ro' casualties caused by water ingress

Date	Vessel	Cause	No. of deaths
1953	Princess Victoria	Weather	13
1966	Heraklion	Weather	21
1966	Skagerak	Weather	
1968	Wahine	Weather	5
1975	Straitsman	Capsize in port	
1976	Sophia	Capsize in port	
1977	Hero	Weather	
1977	Seaspeed Dora	Capsize in port	
1978	Jolly Assuro	Collision	
1980	Tollan	Collision	
1980	Zenobia	Cargo shift	
1981	Sloman Ranger	Collision	
1981	Siboney	Capsize in port	
1982	European Gateway	Collision	
1984	Sundancer	Flooding / Grounding	
1987	Herald of Free Enterprise	Doors open	19
1991	Salem Express	Collision	47
1991	Moby Prince	Collision	14
1993	Jan Heweliusz	Weather	5

Source: Lloyds List, 1994

Table 2
Decline in passenger numbers following Estonia

Operator	Route	No. passengers for Quarter 4 1993	No. passengers for Quarter 4 1994	% ±
Stena	Sweden-Germany	196,800	168,400	-14
TT Line	Sweden-Germany	126,700	123,800	-2
Hansa Ferry	Sweden-Germany	110,500	105,900	-4
Viking Line	Sweden-Finland	283,000	199,100	-30
Viking Line*	Sweden-Finland	383,300	270,100	-30
Silja Line	Sweden-Finland	339,600	329,400	-3
Silja Line*	Sweden-Finland	442,400	434,500	-2
Estline	**Sweden-Estonia**	**68,300**	**11,200**	**-84**

*Alternative ports, same route

Source: Cruise and Ferry, 1995

Although many of the costs may be insured against, there could still be a further increase in the cost of cover. It is difficult to put a precise figure on both the actual and the 'hidden' costs of a ferry accident; suffice to say that these costs are undeniably substantial. It would be interesting then to discover what the cost of improving Ro' Ro' ferry safety and stability is, and how it balances out with the above mentioned costs.

Methods and the cost of change

There are numerous ideas to improve Ro' Ro' ferry safety, which can be categorised into two distinct areas: (i) structural operational measures, most of which concentrate on the key issue of stability and loss prevention; and (ii) organisational based operational changes, which are more concerned with life preservation and loss minimisation following an incident. Many of the structural safety improvements such as internal buoyancy spaces and reverse camber docks are being incorporated in new buildings, but older vessels have to be retrofitted with less costly ideas. The most viable suggestions to date are:

- transverse bulkheads
- external steel sponsons
- rapid pumping drainage tanks

Transverse bulkheads cost approximately £100,000 each and it has been recommended that three bulkheads would provide the optimum protection. Allowing for a one-off time out of service to fit the bulkheads, the capital cost should not exceed more than £400,000. Considering the addition of an extra 5-10 minutes on to journey times, training of crew, intermittent maintenance and a negligible loss in cargo carrying capacity (about 3%), the yearly cost should not have a significant impact on profitability.

External steel sponsons are slightly more expensive with a capital cost of about £600,000. Taking into account an increase in fuel consumption, annual running costs would be slightly higher.

Rapid pumping draining tanks are a practical solution to the problem of water on the deck, but this method should be used in conjunction with transverse bulkheads. Although the precise figure for the fitting of drainage tanks is not yet known, it is not thought that the cost will be more than £500.000.

Individually these improvements are inexpensive; even a combination of, for example, transverse bulkheads and rapid pumping draining tanks could be achieved for less than £1.0 million. Any extra running and maintenance costs could be offset by a minimal increase in fares. Comparing these low costs and the actual cost of an accident, it appears to make sound financial sense for shipowners to implement better safety measures rather than accepting the possibility of an accident and insuring against it. Yet in view of all this information, legislative bodies such as the IMO are slow to impose safety demands, whilst shipowners are reluctant to implement changes of their own accord, the result being that good ideas tend to get sidelined. Some in the shipping industry do not recognise the merit in such improvements and governments are also slow to endorse change. However, it is interesting to note that during the Falklands war in 1982, the Royal Navy retrofitted transverse bulkheads to the Ro' Ro's which they had requisitioned from the commercial shipping sector, and which the Navy operated as soldier/stores carriers. Presumably this was in order to provide the maximum safety to those on board. Evidently, therefore, someone with authority in the Royal Navy must have decided that the cost of temporarily adding transverse bulkheads was at least equal to the benefit that they provided (Crainer, S, 1993, p. 30). The transverse bulkheads were removed from the ferries upon their return to normal commercial sailing.

Suggestions among the organisation base changes include updating some of the legislative bodies such as the Safety of Life at Sea (SOLAS), Standards of Training Certification and Watchkeeping (STCW) and the Search and Rescue Conventions. To some degree SOLAS is being updated with the implementation of the International Safety Management Code (ISM Code) in June 1998. There is also a need to increase the standards of lifesaving equipment and heighten 'spot checks' on passenger ferries.

Developments in the UK and rest of world

New IMO standards require all Ro' Ro' ferries to increase safety standards to a prescribed level by 2005. Some countries have brought this date forward and are implementing these changes as soon as possible; for example, Norway should have completed the changes by 1 May 1996. The UK government do not seem to perceive these standards as a key issue and even though they did bring the date forward by two years to 2003, they argue that bringing the IMO's deadline for changes any further forward would place British operators at a 'competitive disadvantage' against other operators. Whilst this may be an important factor and one which requires due consideration, perhaps a more constructive approach would be to discuss the possibility of offering incentives for early completion, such as government subsidies, tax incentives, grants or interest free loans to help UK operators speed up the implementation of these new standards. This would serve to provide better equipped ships and would in effect increase, rather than decrease, the competitive advantage of UK Ro' Ro' ferry operators.

As a result of the Herald of Free Enterprise incident in 1987, and the following 'Sheen Inquiry' and the 'Sheen Report', new laws are currently being implemented in the UK to make cases of corporate manslaughter easier to bring to court. To some extent this has already taken effect with the successful prosecution and subsequent three year prison sentence of a trawler manager on 14 March 1996 in the recent Pescado case (although subsequently reversed on appeal). This matter of personal accountability for a failure to provide a duty of care, is a fairly radical approach and may again have a positive effect on the eradication of substandard vessels and cause negligent owners to think twice about safety. However, there is a risk of discouraging shipowners from continuing in shipping with such drastic measures coming into force. This would increasingly be the case if shipowners were still liable for corporate manslaughter even when they have exercised due diligence in appointing a respected classification society, who then failed to make the proper representations about the condition and state of the vessel. It may also be the case in larger shipping organisations that 'scapegoats' are offered up for conviction, when in truth the actual fault may rest higher up the corporate ladder.

Conclusion

While ferries have made great technological advances in terms of carrying capacity, liability Conventions and classification societies have remained virtually untouched and safety legislation has been slow to keep up. This paper highlights two main areas of concern. The first being that limitation of liability Conventions, as they currently stand, appear to have a direct causal relationship with the standards of safety on Ro' Ro' passenger ferries. This is because the levels of limitation are not high enough to deter shipowners from operating substandard ships, now are they high enough to force insurers to exert sufficient pressure on shipowners to improve their safety. This flexibility creates a void that can be exploited by certain shipowners. In addition, the flexibility afforded to insurers and P & I Clubs when calculating compensation claims adds to the disenfranchisement of the Convention Articles, leaving them weak and ineffectual. The second area of concern is that classification societies seem to have moved away from their original mandate, and are increasingly making critical decisions on vessel safety on the basis of market forces. At the same time they remain in a virtual 'liability free zone' when it comes to their acts or omissions.

In conclusion, it is apparent that a series of changes need to be implemented in Ro' Ro' ferry operations. It is important to avoid so-called 'knee jerk reactions' following on from the Estonia and similar incidents, but a practical way of minimising the possibility of these incidents in the future requires serious discussion and action. The first step could be to bring all suitable vessels up to the new IMO specifications as soon as possible. This may require the assistance of governments through taxation incentives or loans, but as illustrated, would help to increase the profile of the ferry industry. A review of the liability Conventions and amendments to the deficient Articles would also help to eradicate poor standard vessels. With respect to classification societies, it is believed that they should undergo a complete post-mortem. This is necessary in order to discover if and how the structure could be re-organised and re-defined to cope with new proposals. Changes should be made to classification checks with the view to encompassing a wider area, such as life saving appliances and equipment, crew training and also cargo loading techniques. Comprehensive checks should be made before voyages as is the case in the airline industry. In conjunction with these changes, it would be appropriate to look at the ways in which classification societies could accept more liability for their actions, thus mistakes will be recognised and compensated accordingly. These changes potentially could have a great effect in improving the safety standards of vessels. It is hoped that a certificate of class could become as close to a guarantee of seaworthiness as is possible, ensuring that a particular vessel is safe, from it's crew to it's life saving equipment, and it's hull to the engines. Meanwhile, the reputation of classification societies will be re-established as a thorough body of professionals whose decisions are not determined or influenced by market forces.

Apart from cases of gross negligence, it is not envisaged that shipowners and classification societies should be forced to accept limitless liability claims, nor should they be unnecessarily exposed to charges of corporate manslaughter. This could harm shipping in the future and may not solve any problems. It is more important that the limits are set to a level which serve to compensate adequately the victims of an accident, and that are realistically going to discourage operators from substandard safety. It is important to strike some balance in this area. Sections of the Ro' Ro' ferry sector find themselves in the paradoxical situation where they do not appreciate that by investing in safety and increasing the profile and prestige of Ro' Ro' ferries, customer confidence will rise, passenger throughput will increase, insurance premiums will fall and revenues will show increases. Some operators have adopted this line of thought, and these are the same operators who will continue to compete with the air and tunnel operators.

In order to obtain a more complete, rounded and sustainable level of safety, all involved parties, including insurers, shipowners, ship builders, unions, classification societies and legislators, need to work closely together in setting the right tone for Ro' Ro' ferry shipping into the next millennium. In terms of the Estonia incident, it is difficult to imagine that the cause of the sinking would not have been discovered and that she would not have been permitted to sail, if the classification society would have been held partly or wholly responsible. Indeed, if the liability levels were much more substantial, would the P & I Club not have demanded routine checks prior to each voyage? However, in this instance hindsight is not much use unless it can be used constructively to ensure that similar incidents can not occur again. The reasons for change are available, as are the methods for implementing those changes. All the changes outlined will serve to boost the confidence of passengers, make the industry easier to market in the face of criticism and competition, and provide a solid foundation for future growth, but more importantly it will save lives. All that is required now is positive action.

Postscript

At the time of writing this paper (19 April 1996) neither the crew of the Estonia, nor any of their families have yet received a financial settlement in respect of compensation for loss of life and personal injury. The insurance for the Estonia's hull and machinery, however, was paid in November 1994.

The Swedish and Finnish maritime authorities have begun the task of pouring sand, rocks and concrete over the wreck site of the Estonia at an estimated cost of between $45-$80 million. The reasons given are; to reduce the hazard to other vessels, and to prevent the wreck from being disturbed by divers or thieves. However, as the vessel is resting at over 80 meters of water, it is not a direct hazard to shipping, and it is difficult to get to from a diver's point of view. This action is in contradiction with the wishes of the majority of those relatives who still have deceased members of family in the vessel, and those who also feel that the large amount of money being spent on this venture could be better spent elsewhere. Another effect of 'sealing up' the vessel would be that of suppressing any further evidence should it be required at a later stage of either the court cases.

There are currently two cases being brought to trial by the International Support Group within the two year time bar. The first in Germany against the shipbuilder Meyer becuase of the faulty door locks. The second is being brought in France against the classification society Bureau Veritas for failing to notice that the locks were faulty, and allowing the ship to sail. The latter case, if successful, would be one of the first decisions that has ever gone in favour of punishing a classification society for negligent conduct with respect to a third party. In addition, the number of cases being brought against classification societies is increasing. This pressure, coupled with the decision against a classification society, could prove to be the catalyst for some of the changes proposed in this paper.

The story of the Estonia is not yet finished and the implications surrounding the events on 28 September 1994 will be felt by the Ro' Ro' passenger ferry industry for years to come.

References

Crainer, S (1993), *Zeebrugge, Learning from Disaster*, p. 30, Herald Charitable Trust: London.

Cruise and Ferry 1995, May/June, Lloyds Ship Manager Supplement, pp. 10-12.

Cruise and Ferry Design 91, September, No. 10, p. 115.

Fairplay 1995, 2 November, Vol. 326, Issue 5840, pp. 3-4, 9, 28-29.

Gunnar Bendreus, of the International Support Group.

Leading Developments in International Marine Insurance 1991, pp. 79-81, London Press Ltd: London.

Lloyds List 1994, 29 September, No. 55,844, pp. 1, 3, 15.

Lloyds List 1994, 27 October, No. 55,867, p. 14.

Lloyds List 1994, 21 December, No. 56,225, p. 10.

Lloyds List 1995, 20 April, No. 56,015, p. 10.

Shipping and the Baltic metal trades

Kevin Cullinane and Marius Rostock Olsen
Institute of Marine Studies
University of Plymouth

Abstract

This paper presents a review of the specialised metal trades in the Baltic region. The objectives were to provide:

- An analysis of the non-ferrous metal market in terms of past and present production and of the exports of non-ferrous metal and its impact on the demand for seaborne trade.

- An overview of the transportation chain from source (production plant) to the first destination port in Western Europe, focusing on the issues of transhipment and storage.

Introduction

It is now almost five years since the Soviet Union fragmented, having an immediate effect on the Communist Party and its apparatus of economic control over the whole of the Former Soviet Union (FSU). Since then, several FSU producing nations have emerged as major exporters of various products to the West. The production of non-ferrous metals, such as aluminium, copper, zinc, nickel, lead and tin is extremely energy intensive. As a consequence of cheap domestic energy policies, FSU nations have proved to be competitive with the Western world. The export of these metals from the FSU has, therefore, increased considerably over the past four years (Disraeli, 1995).

The export of ferrous metals has also increased rapidly during the same period. These, however, are exported in much larger shipments and are, therefore, associated with deep-sea rather than short-sea trades.

Until recently very little has been known about the actual trade of non-ferrous metal. Statistics are unreliable when it comes to the production or export of these metals and, since they are seen as strategic and forming part of the military industrial complex, the FSU nations keep their non-ferrous metal production and export statistics secret. There are, of course, some companies which have great knowledge of this trade, but due to commercial confidentiality most of them tend to be very careful with this information.

Almost 75% of all metals coming out of the FSU go out through the Baltic Sea, and the majority of this goes direct to Rotterdam (Parness, 1995). The freight rates paid for this transport are normally very low. This is most probably due to the existence of agreements between some ship owning companies and some of the biggest metal warehouses in Rotterdam (Ross, 1995).

The objective of the research was to undertake a comprehensive analysis of the previous and present logistics strategy for the Baltic non-ferrous metal trade based on the following:

- An analysis of the non-ferrous metal market in terms of past and present production and of the exports of non-ferrous metal and its impact on the demand for seaborne trade.

- An overview of the transportation chain from source (production plant) to the first destination port in Western Europe, focusing on the issues of transhipment and storage.

The scope of the research will be limited to the issues which impact directly on the current situation. In this context, an analysis of the past five years since

1991 is deemed most appropriate. The FSU is unlikely to follow any clear and logical future path. The project will not, therefore, provide extensive coverage of the future prospects of the trade. There are too many uncertainties which make such forecasts unreliable.

The research is constrained to cover any export of non-ferrous metals from the FSU via the Baltic Sea to Rotterdam. Some other geographical areas for export will be discussed, but this will only be done on an ad-hoc basis as appropriate.

The three major non-ferrous metals - aluminium, copper and zinc will be given special attention and will therefore be discussed separately. For the purpose of this work, the others will from now on be discussed en-masse as "other non-ferrous metals".

Some problems were encountered in conducting this research:

- Because of the previous situation in the FSU, characterised by instability, FSU metal statistics were kept secret as they were deemed relevant to the military industries. This has made it very difficult to obtain reliable statistics in this area. Even today, almost four years since the break-up of the FSU, these statistics are difficult to obtain, and even when available are very often not in the form required and/or are unreliable. This research is therefore based on reports produced by independent companies and on port statistics obtained from The Netherlands. Import statistics from individual countries in Europe could not be used, because these very rarely show whether the metals have been transhipped or not.

- The many changes which have taken place in the FSU over the past five years have resulted in a considerable number of different definitions of geographical areas. This has made it extremely and sometimes impossible to compare the various statistics. Very often even public statistics include different geographical areas under the same definition. For this research, it was decided to use the FSU as a general definition.

- Another problem when analysing statistics from this trade, is that some statistics show Poland and the Baltic countries exporting large quantities of metals which, in many cases are actually originating in Russia and the CIS. These countries are used simply as transit routes. For the purpose of this project, these countries are not discussed separately but effectively as a part of the FSU.

Another major problem is that some statistics combine refined metals with metal alloys. This is a problem which in many cases is impossible to discover and will, therefore, influence the statistics later produced.

Historical overview of the non-ferrous metal industry

Since the FSU split apart, what we have witnessed can well be described by the expression from "Marx to Market" (Yergin and Gustafson, 1994). In the past, all metal plants were owned by the Communist Party which exercised overall control and gave commands from its headquarters in Moscow (Gregory and Stuart, 1986).

These metal plants are located in proximity to energy sources such as that, in many cases, raw materials are transported over tremendous distances before reaching the plants where they are smelted. When the product is finished it then has to be transported to customers. This means that the non-ferrous metals industry is very transport intensive, an aspect that will be described in more detail later.

The main reason for this "unwieldy" supply and production chain is the interdependence for the supply of materials of the FSU republics. Nurturing this interdependence was an essential principle of the communist regime in the FSU (Collins and Rodrick, 1991).

With the collapse of the Iron Curtain, the FSU mining and metals industries have produced a number of surprises for Western observers. The growth of the aluminium smelting industry in Siberia had been highly underestimated throughout the 1970s and 1980s, with the result that by 1990, Western estimates of the FSU production, developed by the US Bureau of Mines and Metallgesellschaft of Germany, stood at around 1 million tonnes below what has turned out to be the actual level of production during that period. Production of copper, nickel and tin had also been similarly underestimated (Humphreys, 1994).

The demise of the Soviet Union and its particular form of economic organisation left a unique legacy in the region and posed an enormous challenge to world metal markets, its participants and related sectors, one of which was the short-sea shipping industry.

Recent trends in production and export

Since 1989, the production of the various non-ferrous metals has fallen while the export of these metals has received a boost. The reasons for this are several and consist of a complex web of economic and political factors. Some important reasons, however, should be highlighted:

* The break-up of the FSU resulted in a collapse of domestic (primarily military) demand, which released considerable amounts of metals for export (Roberts and Arlyuk, 1995).

- The disappearance of Soviet command and control left a vacuum which has yet to be filled by efficient market forces. In the mean time, the industry is suffering from a lack of direction (Golman, 1991).

- Essential links between raw material suppliers, manufacturers and end users, often all three being elements of the same military complex, have evaporated leaving local management to pick up the pieces which they were unprepared and unable to do properly (Metallgesellschaft, 1993).

- There has also been a growing energy shortage; this is because most of the FSU's power stations are obsolete and need complete updating. This problem has worsened since four nuclear power plants will not be brought into service as originally planned and other power stations have already reduced their electricity output for safety reasons (Metallgesellschaft, 1993).

- Lack of strength in the FSU currencies makes it difficult to buy raw materials and invest in new production plants, etc. (Collins and Rodrick, 1991). This makes it even more difficult to maintain the same production level as previously was the case. As a result of this lack of finance, it has become necessary to increase exports to obtain hard currency.

- The former organisation and structure of the industry makes little economic sense under the discipline of a free market which has lead to a reduction in the output of the industry (Chu and Schwartz, 1993).

- The transportation chain is longer and more complex and the energy used to produce non-ferrous metals is greater than in many countries in the west. Despite this, the economic situation in the FSU, together with the different system it uses to evaluate production costs, has made the FSU's non-ferrous metal sector very competitive in the Western world (Riiser, 1995). However, as illustrated in Table 1, the sensitivity of very large fixed costs, to changing phases of the economic cycle, and the difficulty in quickly altering production levels in response to demand still creates substantial fluctuations around the average price.

In February 1993, there were major differences in prices between London and Moscow. This situation has now changed, however, and the price gap is now marginal compared with that time. This has resulted in an environment where the metal market makes a profit trading on margins. Obviously, this means that the transportation costs of the commodity have become much more critical than before (Person, 1995).

Table 1
A comparison of non-ferrous metal prices in Moscow and London
(US $ / tonne)

18 February 1993			
Metal	**Moscow**	**London**	**Difference in price**
Aluminium	680	1294	614
Copper	1091	2212	1121
Lead	340	411	71
Nickel	2594	6208	3614
Tin	3131	5785	2654
Zinc	680	1062	382

Source: Humphreys (1994)

The changes which have taken place over the past four or five years have resulted in a considerable increase in the export of non-ferrous metals, with some metals showing a much more significant increase than others.   This section intends to show the changes in production and export which have occurred during the period 1989-1995. Each metal will be analysed separately with the exception of the "other non-ferrous" group which will be discussed as a whole.

Aluminium

Aluminium is by far the most important of the non-ferrous metals in terms of quantities produced and exported. It is, therefore, the most important non-ferrous metal from a shipping point of view.

As can be seen from Table 2, production has fallen from 3.5 million tonnes in 1989 to approximately 2.6 million tonnes in 1995, a reduction of 26%. Production then remained fairly stable over the period 1992 to 1994. In 1995 it dropped some 0.5 million tonnes as a result of the "Memorandum of Understanding" which Russia signed with the Aluminium Association to cut production by this amount.   This was agreed in order to force the price upwards by restoring the market balance within the aluminium industry (Riiser, 1995).

Over the same period, exports have increased from 0.29 million tonnes in 1989 to approximately 2 million tonnes in 1995, representing a growth of 590 per cent.   According to Universal Bulk Transport (UBT), 75% of all aluminium exports move through the Baltic Sea.   This enormous increase in the export of aluminium, therefore, has had a considerable effect on the short-sea shipping industry in the Baltic Sea.

Table 2
FSU aluminium production and exports
(tonnes)

Year	Produc-tion	Exports	Exports to Europe	Imports to Rotter	Imports to Amster	Imports to Nether	O.W. carried in containers	Carried in containers as a % of total imports to Nether	Imports going for storage	Imports trans-shipped	Imports to Rotter as a % of tot. exp. to Europe
1989	3500000	290000	222000	186046	353	186399	3659	1.96 %	0	164626	84 %
1990	3523000	364000	276000	231000	353	231353	3650	1.58 %	0	210000	84 %
1991	3250000	713000	361000	270000	0	270000	2100	0.78 %	0	250000	75 %
1992	3193000	755000	582000	427184	0	427184	2025	0.47 %	373930	51279	73 %
1993	3120000	170000	900000	878190	0	878190	15399	1.75 %	754120	98940	98 %
1994	3080000	210000	110000	1085700	0	1085700	15856	1.46 %	906700	150000	99 %
1995	2580000	200000	100000	980000	0	980000	15000	1.53 %	0	950000	98 %

Source: Riiser (1995), International Lead and Zinc Study Group (1995), Metal Bulletin (1995)

Table 3
Copper production and exports from the FSU
(tonnes)

Year	Produc-tion	Exports	Exports to Europe	Imports to Rotter	Imports to Amster	Imports to Nether	O.W. carried in containers	Carried in containers as a % of total imports to Nether	Imports going for storage	Imports trans-shipped	Imports to Rotter as a % of tot. exp. to Europe
1989	800000	130000	128000	109248	1294	110542	2194	1.98 %	0	110040	86 %
1990	800000	150000	139000	124500	1100	125600	2400	1.91 %	0	125000	90 %
1991	794000	175000	155750	120750	0	120750	2400	1.99 %	0	120500	78 %
1992	683000	170000	153000	96432	75	96507	1934	2.00 %	56116	40162	63 %
1993	570000	450000	430000	305387	120	305507	9487	3.11 %	240768	63947	71 %
1994	573000	470000	440241	312571	230	312801	6000	1.92 %	250000	62500	71 %
1995	591000	320000	400000	280000	100	280100	5000	1.79 %	40000	240000	70 %

Source: Riiser (1995), International Lead and Zinc Study Group (1995), Metal Bulletin (1995)

Copper

From the perspective of seaborne trade, copper is the second most important non-ferrous metal. In terms of tonnes, however, it is much smaller than aluminium.

Copper production has fallen from 0.8 million tonnes in 1989 to approximately 0.591 million tonnes in 1995, a reduction of some 26%. Table 3 shows that during the same period, exports have increased from 0.13 million tonnes to approximately 0.32 million tonnes, representing an increase of some 146%.

At the time of writing, exports are expected to drop from a peak in 1994 of 0.47 million tonnes to 0.32 million tonnes in 1995. This is mainly due to increased domestic demand (Metal Bulletin, 1995).

When it comes to the export of copper from the FSU, it is difficult to say how much of this moves through the Baltic Sea. This will be discussed in detail in a later section.

Zinc

Zinc is the third most important non-ferrous metal in terms of tonnage moved. Zinc production in the FSU has fallen from 0.65 million tonnes in 1989 to approximately 0.37 million tonnes in 1995. This represents a reduction of 43 per cent. During the same period, exports have increase considerably from 18,000 tonnes in 1989 to as much as 0.16 million tonnes in 1994. As can be seen from Table 4, exports look to be 40,000 tonnes less in 1995. From 1989 to 1995, however, exports will have increased by some 566%.

Other non-ferrous metals (nickel, lead and tin)

Nickel, lead and tin are grouped together because FSU production and export of each individually is so small compared to the rest of the world. In the FSU, nickel exports account for some 85% of this group which means that the exports of lead and tin are very small. This has meant that evaluating their potential from a shipping point of view would be very difficult and largely inappropriate.

As shown in Table 5, the production of other non-ferrous metals has actually increased from 0.24 million tonnes in 1989 to 0.25 million tonnes in 1995; and increase of 5%. Exports have increased from 0.17 million tonnes in 1989 to 0.21 million tonnes in 1995, yielding an increase of 26% (International Lead and Zinc Study Group, July 1995).

Table 4
Zinc production and exports from the FSU
(tonnes)

Year	Production	Exports	Exports to Europe	Imports to Rotter	Imports to Amster	Imports to Nether	O.W. carried in containers	Carried in containers as a % of total imports to Nether	Imports going for storage	Imports trans-shipped	Imports to Rotter as a % of tot. exp. to Europe
1989	650000	18000	18000	0	0	0	0	0 %	0	0	0 %
1990	550000	19000	19000	0	0	0	0	0 %	0	0	0 %
1991	500000	5000	5000	0	0	0	0	0 %	0	0	0 %
1992	450000	80000	80000	34266	0	34266	79	0.23 %	32552	1714	43 %
1993	502000	149000	149000	146103	0	146103	15955	10.92 %	92407	38691	100 %
1994	375000	160000	160000	155200	0	155200	17500	11.28 %	99800	39000	97 %
1995	370000	120000	120000	115000	0	115000	13000	11.30 %	55000	45000	96 %

Source: Riiser (1995), International Lead and Zinc Study Group (1995), Metal Bulletin (1995)

Table 5

The production and export of other non-ferrous metals from the FSU
(tonnes)

Year	Production	Exports	Exports to Europe	Imports to Rotter	Imports to Amster	Imports to Nether	O.W. carried in containers	Carried in containers as a % of total imports to Nether	Imports going for storage	Imports trans-shipped	Imports to Rotter as a % of tot. exp. to Europe
1989	237400	166000	136000	100645	103	100748	3772	3.74 %	0	100578	74 %
1990	300000	178000	131000	93700	120	93820	3700	3.94 %	0	93500	72 %
1991	298000	215000	125000	79000	130	79130	3760	4.75 %	0	79100	63 %
1992	293000	244000	132000	69438	148	69586	3406	4.89 %	39122	10368	53 %
1993	274800	229000	215000	189336	190	189526	13667	7.21 %	147861	37189	88 %
1994	261000	238000	218000	192000	210	192210	14200	7.39 %	153768	38300	88 %
1995	251000	210000	190000	160000	230	160230	3500	2.18 %	30000	130000	84 %

Source: Rüser (1995), International Lead and Zinc Study Group (1995), Metal Bulletin (1995)

Location of plants

Most non-ferrous metals are transported over considerable distances within the FSU before being loaded onto ships in the Baltic Sea. As a result, plant locations are very inefficient from a transportation point of view. Reasons for their location can, however, be summarised as follows:

• Because metals were an important part of the military effort, during World War II Stalin desired to have the metal plants as far from the battle areas as possible (Bush, 1994).

• A similar strategy was followed during the post-war period, because the communist party wanted to increase the economic interdependency of the various republics in order to quell any moves towards political independence.

• Sources of energy were seen as a more important factor than transportation when making decisions about where a plant should be located.

Due to this strategy, the FSU contains an extensive network of railways. Although rates have increased recently and despite the distances involved in transportation, transport costs are still low enough to make the FSU non-ferrous metals competitive in the Western world (Bohner, 1993).

Table 6 shows the distribution of non-ferrous metal production among the Republics of the FSU. This is followed by an in-depth analysis of the transportation of individual metals.

Table 6
Percentage distribution of non-ferrous metals among the Republics of the FSU

Refined metal	Russia	Kazakhs-tan	Ukraine	Uzbekis-tan	Tajikis-tan	Total
Alumin	83%	2%			15%	100%
Copper	60%	32%		8%		100%
Zinc	33%	46%	2%	19%		100%
Nickel	99%		1%			100%
Lead	10%	90%				100%
Tin	100%					100%

Source: Humphreys (1994)

Aluminium

Approximately 60% of all aluminium production in the FSU (a total of 1.6 million tonnes) comes from the two large plants at Bratsk (the world's largest) and at Krasnoyarsk (Riiser, 1995). These two plants are located in the middle of the FSU which means that aluminium produced for export has to be transported over thousands of kilometres by rail before reaching either a loading port or a final consumer.

According to UBT, the main carrier of aluminium from the FSU, 75% of all aluminium moves through the Baltic Sea. According to the rail research department of UBT, the average time aluminium spends on this rail network before reaching any Baltic port is approximately three to four weeks (Parness, 1995). Due to commercial confidentiality, nothing is said about rail freight rates, except that they are very cheap compared with those in the Western world. Nearly all aluminium which is exported through Baltic seaports goes either via St Petersburg or Ventspiels. The reasons for this are:

- The very good railway network which connects these two ports with the rest of the FSU.

- Trans-World Metals, one of the world's largest metal traders, own and have agreements with some of the terminals in these two ports.

- Ventspiels has no ice problems during the winter.

Copper

In 1994, the FSU produced 0.57 million tonnes of copper. Of this, 0.31 million tonnes (55%) were produced by the Norilsk copper and nickel plant in north Siberia (Metal Bulletin, 1995). The quality of Norilsk copper meets the requirements of the London Metal Exchange (LME) which means it has a very high copper content and is, therefore considered good quality (Ikonnikov, 1993). As a result, the copper produced by the Norilsk plant is most likely to go for export to Western countries.

The Norilsk plant is located along the river "Yeniseyskiy Zaliv" which runs into the Arctic Ocean. The port use is Dudinca which is connected by railway to the Norilsk plant. Dudinca can take ships as big as 10,000 d.w.t. which, because of the long distance to Europe, is close to the average size of shipment. Because of the difficult weather conditions in this area, however, most of the copper is transported down to the Baltic Sea by rail to be loaded onto ships.

Nearly 100% of all copper which goes out of Dudinca by ship is either carried by Murmansk Shipping or by the Northern Shipping Company (based in Archangel in Russia), both of which have an agreement with the Norilsk plant. Murmansk Shipping are able to ship copper out of Dudinca during the winter as they have icebreakers, though these are old and poorly maintained and, therefore, very often out of action (Ross, 1995).

For normal (not ice classed) dry bulk carriers, the season in this area is very short (middle of June to the beginning of October). The season starts so late because there is a lot of ice melting in this area. During the spring, the river "Yeniseyskiy Zaliv" increases its depth by some two to three metres making it impossible to load at the berth in Dudinca (Bastesen, 1995). The crane systems are even dismantled during the spring, in order to prevent them being damaged (Casteberg, 1995). Taking the above factors into account, it would seem possible that a lot of the copper is transported by rail down to the Baltic Sea. The only problem is that no railway connects the Norilsk plant with the rest of Russia. This means that it has to be transported by lorry to Murmansk before being transhipped onto rail (Baker, 1995).

The rest of the FSU copper production is located in the Urals region at the four main enterprises there (Gai, Krasnouralsk, Sredneuralsk and Mednogorsk) with a total production of approximately 0.18 million tonnes (Burstein, 1995). From these enterprises it takes approximately two or three weeks by rail to reach the Baltic ports (Pearn, 1995).

Nearly 100% of the copper which goes out through the Baltic Sea moves through St Petersburg. This is mainly due to the good railway network connecting this port with North Russia. St Petersburg also has some very good and safe storage warehouses which is very important because of the high value of copper (Ezendam, 1995).

Zinc

The majority (approximately 0.125 million tonnes) of the zinc produced in the FSU is produced in the Urals region with Gai as the largest smelter. The transport of zinc is therefore similar to that of copper.

As was seen in Table 4, Kazakhstan accounts for approximately 45% of the total zinc production. This equates to 0.17 million tonnes. The whereabouts of these mines has proved difficult to determine but the average transport time by rail from the north-west border of Kazakhstan is approximately three weeks (Baker, 1995), which means that zinc transport is something between three and four weeks. The main ports used in the Baltic Sea are St Petersburg and Kaliningrad (Karlsen, 1995).

As much as 0.18 million tonnes (70%) of all nickel produced in the FSU is from the Norilsk plant in North Siberia (Salathiel, 1990). For further information about this plant see the copper section above. As the tonnage involved is much smaller than that of copper, the shipments are naturally smaller.

As the value of nickel is extremely high ($10,000 a tonne) (London Metal Exchange, 1995), it is very expensive to keep it in storage. The nickel is, therefore, more likely to be transported in much smaller shipments. This is especially the case nowadays when these plants are in urgent need for capital investment.

Due to the small quantities of nickel, more are likely to go on rail from Dudincia than copper; however some of the nickel will also be shipped as a part cargo when carrying copper. However, the quantities of lead and tin are so small that they present few interesting issue to be discussed.

When these metals reach any Baltic port they normally go into storage whilst waiting for a ship to carry them to the continent (Rotterdam). Depending upon the availability of ships for aluminium, the average storage time is approximately seven to 14 days in St Petersburg and Ventspiels (Parness, 1995). When it comes to other metals, we can expect approximately the same storage time for full cargoes, but shorter storage time for those consignments which are going to be part cargoes.

Normally, free storage is offered as long as the warehouse does the cargo handling. As non-ferrous metals are very expensive they need to be keep secure for as long as they are stored. This service is not included in the storage agreement and is, therefore, charged extra.

Exports to Rotterdam

As has already been noted, nearly 100% of all non-ferrous metal which is exported from the FSU to Europe goes direct to Rotterdam for transhipment or storage. The most important reasons for this are:

• Rotterdam is by far the largest port in Europe in terms of tonnage and ship arrivals. This has resulted in Rotterdam developing a highly efficient distribution network which makes it easy for traders to distribute their commodities further (Ocean Shipping Consultants Ltd, 1995).

• In the past, the agents normally expected the metal traders to contact them. This has now changed and the two main metal warehouses, Steinweg and

H. Hoogerwerff, now work in exactly the opposite way. They now contact the trader direct and give him an offer to get the metals into their warehouse (Pratley, 1995).

- Since 1992, Trans-World Metals have acquired shares of around one third of Russia's four largest aluminium smelters (Ocean Shipping Consultants Ltd, 1995). This has made it the largest trader in Russian aluminium, and according to UBT (a part of Trans-World Metals) they have a very close relationship with Steinweg.

- It is important for the traders to get the metals into a London Metal Exchange warehouse because that allows them to trade it on the LME (at a better price). However, to get the metal into a LME warehouse requires that the metal meets the requirements set by the LME. The non-LME metals can only be traded physically (Baker, 1995).

- Even in the case of a non-LME registered consignment of metals, it is an advantage to get it to Rotterdam. This is because the good distribution network leads to better prices being obtained. There is a tendency, however, towards non-LME metals going direct to consumers rather than to Rotterdam.

Cargo handling

Only a very small proportion of non-ferrous metals are carried in containers. The reasons are several:

- The consignments are normally of such a size that carriage in containers would be very uneconomic.

- Non-ferrous metals are not liable to damage due to the weather.

- Due to the previous political and economic situation in the FSU, there is a lack of infrastructure which facilitates containerisation.

- Due to the small amount of other goods which are carried in containers, very few container ships will usually enter the ports in the area in question. This means it may be difficult to ship it out if containerised.

Aluminium

Aluminium is a relatively light metal. It is normally carried as slabs or ingots which are usually strapped together in bundles of 500 kg. to 1,000 kg.. In most cases, these are loaded on board the ship in two or three bundles nest together (weighing approximately 3,000 kg. in total) which means that heavy cranes are not required (Bishup, 1995). It is important that the loading is done properly in order not to delay discharge unnecessarily and thus incurring demurrage. Recently, a cargo of 3,000 tonnes of loose aluminium ingots which was loaded in two days, took seven days to discharge because of improper loading (Dore, 1995).

The average size per shipment of aluminium out of the Baltic Sea is between 5,000 and 10,000 tonnes. The largest shipment of aluminium ever made out of the Baltic Sea was a vessel of 30,000 d.w.t. with 25,000 tonnes of aluminium loading at St Petersburg for discharge in Rotterdam (Dore, 1995).

As aluminium is moved in relatively large shipments, most of it is carried as a full cargo (Dore, 1995).

Copper

Copper is a very valuable metal ($2,900 / tonne) (Financial Times, 1995) and it should, therefore, be carefully tallied and watched when loaded and discharged to prevent pilferage.

Anodes, Cathodes, Slabs and Blisters are most likely to be transported in bundles of 1,200 mm × 900 mm × 200 mm (920 kg. to 1,500 kg.) stowing at 0.34 cubic metres per tonne. This cargo should be over-stowed with other goods immediately after loading in order to minimise the risk of loss (Thomas, 1989).

Copper is a fairly heavy metal, and any local concentrations of weight should, therefore, be positioned adjacent to the walls where greatest floor strength prevails. It is also essential to provide sufficient shocking off (nailing timber dunnage to the floor, etc..) to prevent even the smallest movement during voyage (Clements, 1995).

As copper is such a valuable cargo it tends to be exported in fairly small shipments of 1,500 to 3,000 tonnes. Copper moves, therefore, more as part cargo than as full cargo (Gerla, 1995). Nevertheless, there are exceptions to this. The copper that moves out of Dudinca by vessel, for example, is transported in large lots of 7,000 to 10,000 tonnes (Ivanron, 1995).

Zinc

Zinc is often referred to as "spelter". It is transported as ingots and, in most cases, is strapped together in bundles of between 350 kg. and 1,000 kg. It is also relatively common, however, for it to be moved on pallets. At the total tonnage of zinc exported is relatively low compared with that of aluminium and copper, nearly all zinc is moved as a part cargo.

Nickel

Nickel is by far the most expensive of the non-ferrous metals and it is, therefore, highly liable to pilferage. Nickel consignments should, therefore, be carefully watched and tallied when loaded and discharged. The cargo should be over-stowed immediately after loading in order to minimise risks.

Due to its extremely high value, all of it is moved in very small consignments which means all nickel is moved as part cargoes. In most cases, nickel is transported in containers, but due to poor container handling systems in the FSU only 7 per cent of it is shipped in containers.

The nickel which goes out through the Baltic Sea and Dudinca is normally transported in drums of 200 - 400 kg., which again are unitised into pallets of four drums with a total weight of no more than 1,500 kg. (Corcisnikov, 1995).

Lead and tin

As the tonnage of lead and tin are so small, it is inappropriate to describe the cargo handling here, as it will vary considerably depending on the size of the shipment.

Factors affecting the freight rates for the non-ferrous metals industry

The main factors which influence the freight rates in this particular trade for this particular area are:

Season

The Baltic Sea is much affected by ice in the winter season as all the rivers and the lakes in the area are frozen (Dore, 1995). Ships tend, therefore, to concentrate in limited accessible areas and the result of this is an increased supply of ships in the Baltic Sea during the winter. In most circumstances this would result in lower freight rates. However, as most of these vessels are restricted by the hull insurance implications of the Institute Warranty Limits

(IWL) they are restricted from going outside the limits given, which are 75 degrees north and 60 degrees south. This is approximately equivalent to Bergen in Norway and Brest in Brittany (Derick, 1995).

The reason for these restrictions are the ice and heavy weather conditions which prevail in this particular area at that time of the year. These restrictions can, however, be lifted by taking out extra hull insurance as this allows them to break the IWL (Gerla, 1995). Not every company can afford this extra expense, and quite often the risk involved in doing so is perceived as too big and the costs, therefore, are considered uneconomical.

Most of these ships to which this scenario is applicable are relatively small and, therefore, this situation is not relevant to deep-sea trading.

Overall, there is a small decrease in freight rates during the winter, but the decrease is not as big as it would have been under normal circumstances given the large amount of ships available in this area in this particular season.

Part cargo versus full cargo

Although not always the case, because a lot of non-ferrous metals move in small quantities, they are shipped as part cargoes. When a consignment is carried as a part cargo it normally pays a higher freight rate, but this is not necessarily the case if it is loaded at the same berth as the rest of the cargo.

If the consignment is large enough to be carried as a full cargo, in most circumstances this is cheaper per unit carried than as a part cargo. This will, however, depend upon the state of the short-sea market compared with that for deep sea. This basically means that if the short-sea market has inordinately high freight rates it might be cheaper to ship it as a part cargo on a deep sea ship (Gerla, 1995). Thus if the consignments are going to somewhere distant then it is most likely to be carried as a part cargo, even if it is large enough to be carried as a full cargo on a small dry bulk carrier. The reason for this is that small dry bulk carriers are suited to short-sea trading and are, therefore, uneconomical on longer journeys.

One berth versus two berths

Due to the high value of the various non-ferrous metals, it is not uncommon that there is more than one owner of the same consignment. This often affects discharge of the cargo because this requires that the consignment is split and then discharged at separate berths. This obviously increases the handling costs and the time taken which, in turn, will increase the freight rates charged.

Private berths versus non-private berths

If the loading berth in the FSU is privately owned then the risk involved is much higher and insurance increases considerably. This obviously affects freight rates (Parness, 1995).

Loading and discharging terms 1

The speed of loading and discharging is naturally very important for the freight rate, and this will, of course, depend upon individual port facilities and the form of the cargo (i.e., barrels, pallets, etc.).

However, the charterer or the shipper usually fixes on a basis of 1,000 tonnes SHEX loading, although the cargo (metal) is thus loaded quite quickly, congestion is still common in FSU ports. When discharged in Rotterdam, the charterer will again fix on the basis of 1,000 tonnes or perhaps 1,500 tonnes SHEX, but in practice 3,000 tonnes should easily be discharged in one day (Gerla, 1995).

Loading and discharging terms 2

If there is no fixed loading time then most of the metals are normally loaded on Customary Quick Despatch (CQD) terms which means that there is no demurrage or despatch involved in the loading port. The shipowner then runs the risk of spending extra time in the loading port. Under such circumstances, it is important that the shipowner makes contact with the port or the agent, in order to check whether the port is an efficient and quick port with good cargo handling systems, and that the cargo is on the quay at the arrival of the ship. When the contract is fixed on CQD terms, it is common that the shipowner contacts the port direct and agrees to pay the agent, for example, an extra $1 a tonne in order to ensure the quickest loading possible. This is, of course, in order to avoid any unnecessary lay time. Under normal conditions the charterer is best off with normal fixed terms, because then there is no need to pay the extra freight costs which the owner would require for fixing on CQD terms.

However, due to conditions in the FSU, it is difficult to know for sure what the situation is going to be when loading. Taking this into account, charterers are often better off with CQD terms since this enables them to hedge against any further costs, such as demurrage and lost freight.

In the case when the shipowner (e.g., UBT or Murmansk Shipping) has an individual agreement with a specific port, there is no more risk when fixing on CQD terms than on fixed terms. This means that freight rates do not necessarily include a premium when fixing on such terms. The result of this is that other owners who do not have such individual agreements lose out if they do not reduce their freight rates.

As discharging is normally carried out on the continent (Rotterdam) and there are very few uncertainties and, therefore, little risk involved, it is nearly always carried out on fixed terms. On the continent most of the ports discharge very quickly and the cargo is often discharged faster than agreed. By custom, however, "short-sea" fixtures are normally concluded on the basis of free despatch (Gerla, 1995).

Export to Rotterdam in relation to transhipment and storage and its effect on the freight rates

Up until 1991, before the changes in the FSU took place, nearly all non-ferrous metals were transhipped immediately, but from late 1991 and up until 1994, approximately 80% of all imports of these metals went into storage at either Steinweg's or H. Hoogerweff's metal warehouse.

Close to 3 million tonnes went into storage during 1993 and 1994. This resulted in the fact that the metal warehouses in Rotterdam generated considerable revenues during that time from storage, while in the past they used to make their money on cargo handling rather than storage. This has now changed, with the result that the metal warehouses on the continent have stared to compete much more than before. This competition has resulted in lower handling costs, though this can be recovered through storage. Because Steinweg and Hoogerwerff are the biggest organisations in this market place, they are able to compete much better than other metal warehouses.

The outcome of this is that the large warehouses have started to make agreements with the most powerful traders such as Universal Bulk Transport in order to make sure that they retain the cargo. These agreements include large discounts on handling, but the discount will, of course, depend upon the size of the trader in terms of tonnage. Large traders would, however, obtain lower storage costs than a small trader.

Another way that the same result might be achieved is by subsidising freight rates. This is normally done in two ways:

1. The metal warehouse makes an agreement with a shipowning company to carry the consignment at a freight rate which is below that of the market. In return, the metal warehouse have to commit themselves to paying the shipowning company some of the storage money. There is, of course, a risk involved with this. If the shipowner agrees, then there is a loss on the freight, which means that this money has to be earned back on storage. If this cargo is sold quickly, then there is not going to be any money

generated by storage of that particular consignment, meaning that this (reduced freight) money is lost.

2. The metal warehouse agrees with the trader to pay some of the freight costs which means that, in this case, it is the warehouse that faces the risk.

The above agreements have a sizeable effect on the freight rates as there is a transfer of margins which results in lower freight rates. As a lot of non-ferrous metals are transported as part cargo, this type of arrangement not only affects the metals themselves but also the cargo which is carried with it.

Documentation in relation to the quality chain

As transportation distances within the FSU are enormous and the political and economic situation is unstable compared with that in the Western world, traders normally buy the metals on FOB contracts. Recently, there has also been increasing Mafia activity in the FSU which makes this inland activity even more risky. This means that the seller is responsible for the transportation within the FSU until it is loaded on board the ship. If the seller does not ship the good FOB then a considerable risk is taken, meaning that extra insurance has to be taken out at a very high cost. As a result, this is very rarely done.

Age of the ship

The fact that non-ferrous metals are so valuable means that it is important that the vessel is not getting too old as this will affect the insurance costs and then the freight rates. The ship should, therefore, not exceed the age of 15 years as insurance costs increase considerably after that age (Parness, 1995).

Conclusion

The objective of this paper was to undertake a comprehensive analysis of the previous and present logistics strategies of the Baltic non-ferrous metal trade. The intent is to determine whether there is any potential for capturing some of the shipping opportunities.

At the moment, there are individual agreements between the parties involved and, for this reason, freight rates are artificially low. By determining the volume of trade and the pattern it takes, it is possible to evaluate the potential for new entrants to make similar agreements.

The analysis carried out clearly shows that exports of non-ferrous metals out of the Baltic Sea, have increased extensively during the past five years, and that most of the exports go direct to the metal warehouses in Rotterdam.

Providing that the export volume stays stable and the destination area remains the same, it is reasonable to believe that individual agreements with metal warehouses in the area could be commercially viable.

Aluminium and copper are the only two metals which have large enough volumes worth considering. The remaining non-ferrous metals have much smaller volumes and, therefore, their regularity of shipments makes them inappropriate for such agreements. Due to the many changes which have taken place in the region during the time period in question, the FSU states are unlikely to follow any clear path in the future. Long term agreements will, therefore, be highly risky and are not to be recommended.

In addition, the uncertainty surrounding the future of the FSU means that long-term agreements of this type are also highly risky.

References

Baker, K. (1995), Trans-World Metals, London.

Bastesen, W. (1995), Jebsens Carriers, Norway.

Bishup, M. (1995), Jebsens, London.

Bohner, H. O. (1993), Aluminium Smelters in the Former USSR. Paper prepared on the request of the European Aluminium Association.

Burstein, M. (1995), *Russia's Copper Industry*, Infomine UK.

Bush, K. (1994), *Aspects of Military Conversion in Russia.*

Casteberg, R, (1992), *The Economics of Murmansk*, The Fridtjof Nansen Institute, Norway.

Chu, K. and Schwartz, G. (1993), Output decline and government expenditures, *Output* Decline *in Eastern Europe - Prospects for Recovery?* Austria.

Clements, D. (1995), Jebsens, London.

Collins, S. M. and Rodrick, D. (1991), *Eastern Europe and the Soviet Union in the World Economy*, Institute of International Economics: Washington D.C.

Corcisnikov, V. (1995), Normaco Ltd, London.

Disraeli, B. (1995), *Key Issues Underlying the Evolution of the Base Metals Industry in the Former Soviet Union*, Brook Hunt & Associates: London.

Dore, K. (1995), Universal Bulk Transport, London.

Gerla, V. (1995), Jebsens, London.

Gerla, V. and Alvsaker, S. (1995), Jebsens, London.

Ezendam, D. J. (1995), Port of Flushing, The Netherlands.

Financial Times (6 September 1995).

Golman, M. (1991), *What went wrong with Perestroika?* Norton: New York.

Gregory, P. R. and Stuart, R. C. (1986), *Soviet Economic Structure and Performance*, Harper and Row: New York.

Humphreys, D. (1994), *Mining and Metals in the CIS, Between Autarky and Integration*, The Royal Institute of International Affairs.

Ikonnikov, V. V. (1993), SGS Vostock, Moscow, Russia.

International Lead and Zinc Study Group (July 1995), Lead and Zinc Statistics.

Ivanron, Y. (1995), Jebsens, Bergen.

Karlsen, L. F. (1995), Fearnleys, Oslo, Norway.

London Metal Exchange (6 January 1995).

Metal Bulletin (1995), Review of the MB's 8th International Copper Conference.

Metallgesellschaft, A. G. (1993), *Development trends of the non-ferrous metals industry in Eastern Europe*.

Ocean Shipping Consultants Ltd (1995), *East Europe & FSU: Trade & Shipping Prospects to 2005*, Guildford.

Parness, V. (1995), Universal Bulk Transport, London.

Pearn, M. (1995), Transportation in the FSU. MB's 2nd Metals of the CIS Conference, Moscow.

Person, U. (1995), AIOC Metal Traders, London.

Pratley, D. (1995), International Commodity Services Ltd, London.

Riiser, M. D. (1995), *Dumping production and exports of aluminium from Russia*, The Royal Institute of International Affairs.

Roberts, H. and Arlyuk, B. (1995), Brook Hunt & Associates, London.

Ross, M. (1995), Jebsens, London.

Salathiel, P. (1990), *Alloy Metals & Steel Market Research*, Heinz H. Pariser, East Germany.

Thomas, R. E. (1989), Thomas' Stowage, *The Properties and Stowage of Cargoes*, Glasgow.

Yergin, D. and Gustafson, T. (1994), Russia 2010.